my **revis**

Edexcel (B) GCSE
SCHOOLS
HISTORY
PROJECT

SECOND EDITION

Sally Thorne
Dan Hartley

HODDER
EDUCATION
AN HACHETTE UK COMPANY

The Publishers would like to thank the following for permission to reproduce copyright material:

Photo credits p. 27 Mary Evans Picture Library/Alamy; **p. 30** © SSPL via Getty Images; **p. 32** © russelljsmith/http://www.flickr.com/photos/russelljsmith/22011649/sizes/o/ http://creativecommons.org/licenses/by/2.0/; **p. 35** © Wellcome Library, London. Wellcome Images/http://creativecommons.org/licenses/by/4.0/; **p. 54** © Punch Limited/TopFoto; **p. 56** © Wellcome Library, London. Wellcome Images/http://creativecommons.org/licenses/by/4.0/; **p. 57** © Gina Sanders – Fotolia; **p. 65** Courtesy of the US Army Medical Department Office of Medical History; **p. 67** *l* © From the Archives of the Royal College of Surgeons of England, *r* © Hulton Archive/Getty Images; **p. 76** © Bettmann/Corbis; **p. 78** © Library of Congress Prints and Photographs Division (LC-USZ62-89570); **p. 81** © The Granger Collection, NYC/TopFoto; **p. 86** © Sally Thorne; **p. 91** *l* X1955.01., *Laugh Kills Lonesome;* Charles M. Russell; Oil on Canvas, 1925 © Courtesy of the Montana Historical Society, Mackay Collection, *r* © Superstock; **p. 119** © 2010 Mary Evans Picture Library; **p. 124** © Bundesarchiv, Plak 003-002-046, Graphiker: René Ahrlé.

Acknowledgements Thanks to Pearson Education Limited (Edexcel) for granting permission to reproduce exam questions. Edexcel accepts no responsibility whatsoever for the accuracy or method of working in the model exam answers given.

Every effort has been made to trace all copyright holders, but if any have been inadvertently overlooked the Publishers will be pleased to make the necessary arrangements at the first opportunity.

Although every effort has been made to ensure that website addresses are correct at time of going to press, Hodder Education cannot be held responsible for the content of any website mentioned in this book. It is sometimes possible to find a relocated web page by typing in the address of the home page for a website in the URL window of your browser.

Hachette Livre UK's policy is to use papers that are natural, renewable and recyclable products and made from wood grown in sustainable forests. The logging and manufacturing processes are expected to conform to the environmental regulations of the country of origin.

Orders: please contact Bookpoint Ltd, 130 Milton Park, Abingdon, Oxon OX14 4SB. Telephone: (44) 01235 827720. Fax: (44) 01235 400454. Lines are open 9.00–5.00, Monday to Saturday, with a 24-hour message answering service. Visit our website at www.hoddereducation.co.uk

© Sally Thorne and Dan Hartley
First published in 2013 by
Hodder Education,
An Hachette UK Company
338 Euston Road
London NW1 3BH

This second edition first published 2014

Impression number   10 9 8 7 6 5 4 3 2
Year   2018 2017 2016 2015 2014

Cover photo © The Gallery Collection/Corbis
Artwork by Datapage (India) Pvt. Ltd.
Typeset in 11/13 Frutiger LT Std by Integra Software Services Pvt. Ltd., Pondicherry, India
Printed in Spain

A catalogue record for this title is available from the British Library

ISBN: 978 1471 83181 2

How to get the most from this book

This book will help you revise for:

- the Development Study (Medicine and Treatment)
- the Historical Source Enquiry (Surgery) and
- the Depth Study (either The American West c1840–c1895 or Life in Germany c1919–c1945)

for the Edexcel (B) GCSE Schools History Project specification.

Use the revision planner on pages 4 and 5 to track your progress, topic by topic. Tick each box when you have:

1. revised and understood each topic
2. answered the exam practice questions
3. checked your answers online.

☑ **Tick to track your progress**

Key term

Key terms are **highlighted** in the section colour the first time they appear, with an explanation nearby in the margin. As you work through this book, highlight other key ideas and add your own notes. Make this **your** book.

☑ **Tick to track your progress as you revise each element of the key content.**

Revision task

Use these tasks to make sure that you have understood every topic and to help you record the key information about each topic.

There are also quick quizzes to test your knowledge of each topic at **www.myrevisionbutton.co.uk/myrevisionnotes**

6 Medicine and treatment c1900 to present day

6.1 New drugs: from prevention to cure

The start of the twentieth century must have been a very exciting time to be in the medical profession. Jenner had shown that vaccination could work; now Pasteur had shown how. Thanks to Pasteur's germ theory, people finally understood what caused disease and this helped with research aimed at tackling it.

To start with, there was a lot of focus on prevention of disease by developing new vaccines. These were particularly aimed at diseases which affected children, such as diphtheria and whooping cough. The government's insistence on vaccinating the population against smallpox meant people began to see the value of vaccination, too.

Scientists also began to develop cures for people who had already been infected. This led to the discovery of the first antibiotics and the growth of the pharmaceutical industry.

Key content
- Further development of vaccines
- Magic bullets and their impact on medical treatments
- How penicillin was discovered and developed

Further development of vaccines

We have already seen how Pasteur and Koch competed with each other at the end of the nineteenth century **to see who could create the most vaccinations**. This rivalry led to huge leaps forward in medical knowledge with the development of new vaccines.

Many of the diseases that were the scourge of the population at the start of the twentieth century are now no longer a problem in the UK, thanks to the development of vaccines. For example, in 1913 Behring managed to produce a vaccine for diphtheria by isolating the anti-toxins produced by the body to fight disease.

As the century progressed, vaccinations were developed for other killers such as tetanus, whooping cough, polio and measles. This led to a decrease in rates of child mortality.

Exam tip
To remind you:
A **vaccination** prevents you getting a disease. It does not cure you if you have already got it.
A **magic bullet** is a chemical drug that cures you when you have already got a disease.

Revision task
In the section on Jenner there was a reminder to look at the long-term and short-term impact of his work (see page 35). The information above could fit into long-term impact! Go back and add to your medical megastar revision card for Jenner to help you remember the long-term impact of his work.

Exam practice
1. How important for the prevention of disease was Edward Jenner's discovery of a smallpox vaccination in 1796? **(12 marks)**

Answers online

Exam tip
When you are answering this question, you will need to look at both the short-term and long-term impact of Jenner's work. Now you have seen how other people built on his discovery, you should be in a better position to explain his importance in the long term.

Magic bullets and their impact on medical treatments

After the discoveries of Pasteur and Koch, their research teams and other scientists, inspired by their work, focused on developing **cures** for major diseases. In addition to this, further research in chemistry and improved government funding led to discoveries which had a huge impact on medical treatment. These factors led to the development of the first chemical cures, or magic bullets.

Key term
Magic bullets – chemical drugs which only killed the disease without affecting the person.

Science and technology – new scientific discoveries improved medical understanding.

Government – more willing to fund medical research.

Exam practice
2. The table below shows two new medical treatments. Choose one and describe the key features of its development.
- Salvarsan 606
- Prontosil **(6 marks)**

Answers online

Magic bullet 1: Salvarsan 606	Magic bullet 2: Prontosil
- Developed by Paul Ehrlich and his research team in 1909	- Developed by Gerhard Domagk in 1932
- Funded by the government	- Attacked the microbes which caused blood poisoning
- Combined dye with various chemicals to target only disease-causing microbes	- He was forced to test his compound on his own daughter who was dying from a pinprick on her finger – luckily it worked
- The 606th compound tested was discovered to be effective by Dr Hata, a member of the research team	- The active ingredient of Prontosil was isolated: sulphonamide
- This was very important: it was the first time chemical drugs had been used to cure illnesses	- Other sulphonamide drugs were developed to cure pneumonia, scarlet fever and meningitis

How penicillin was discovered and developed

- An **antibiotic** is a drug used to treat infections caused by bacteria.
- Salvarsan 606 was the first successful chemical cure which targeted certain diseases. However, antibiotics are not created using chemicals but are produced by **micro-organisms**. Unlike Salvarsan 606, antibiotics can be used on a range of diseases. They use one sort of micro-organism to attack the harmful ones.
- The first antibiotic to be discovered and developed was **penicillin**, a naturally occurring mould. The timeline on page 50 shows how the properties of penicillin were discovered, and then developed into a cure.

Exam tip

Throughout the book there are exam tips that explain how you can boost your final grade.

Exam practice

Sample exam questions are provided for each topic. Use them to consolidate your revision and practise your exam skills.

Answers online

Go online to check your answers to the exam questions at **www.therevisionbutton.co.uk/myrevisionnotes**.

Contents and revision planner

Introduction: Revision and exam technique

Revision technique

We all learn in different ways and if you're going to be successful in your revision you need to work out the ways that work best for you. A good way to begin is to think back to a lesson that you remember in lots of detail. What sort of tasks did you do: reading, writing, role play, discussion? Were you working alone or with other people? Did you ask lots of questions or make lots of notes? What time of day was it: early morning, mid-morning, afternoon? Was it a competition or a timed challenge, or were you working at your own pace?

Use the information to help you build up some strategies to help you revise. Remember that revision doesn't have to be dull and last for hours at a time – but it is really important you do it! The highest grades are awarded to students who have consistently excellent subject knowledge and this only comes with solid revision.

Method 1: 'Brain dumps'

These are particularly useful when done every so often – it's never too early to start! Take a big piece of paper or even a whiteboard and write down everything you can remember about the topic you are revising, one of the units or even the whole History course. You could write down:

● dates
● names of key individuals
● key events or inventions
● important place names
● anything else you can remember.

Once you're satisfied you can't remember anymore, use different colours to highlight or underline the words in groups. For example, you might choose to

underline all the mentions that relate to causes of disease in red, and all the key individuals in blue.

You could extend this task by comparing your brain dump with that of a friend. The next time you do it, try setting yourself a shorter time limit and see if you can write down more.

Method 2: Learning walks

Make use of your space! Write down key facts and place them around your home, where you will see them every day. Make an effort to read the facts whenever you walk past them. This is particularly useful with the development study: each room of your home can represent a different time period. You might decide to put information on the Romans in the loo, for example, since they were so obsessed with public health!

Studies have shown that identifying certain facts with a certain place can help them stick in your mind. So, when you get into the exam room and you find you have a question on Renaissance medicine, you can close your eyes and picture that factsheet on your living room wall ... what does it say?

Method 3: 'Distilling'

Memory studies show that we retain information better if we revisit it regularly. This means that revising the information once is not necessarily going to help it stay in your brain. Going back over the facts at intervals of less than a week leads to the highest retention of facts.

To make this process streamlined, try 'distilling' your notes. Start by reading over the notes you've completed in class or in this revision guide; two days later, read over them again, and this time write down everything you didn't remember. If you repeat this process enough you will end up with hardly any facts left to write down, because they will all be stored in your brain, ready for the exam!

Method 4: Using your downtime

There are always little pockets of time through the day which aren't much good for anything: bus journeys, queues, ad breaks in TV programmes, waiting for the bath to run and so on. If you added all these minutes up it would probably amount to quite a lot of time, and it can be put to good use for revision.

Instead of having to carry around your notes, though, make use of something you carry around with you already. Most of us have a phone that can take pictures and record voice memos, or an iPod or something similar.

- Photograph key sections of this book and read over them.
- Record yourself reading information so that you can listen back over it – while you're playing football, before you go to sleep, or any other time.
- Access the quizzes that go with this book at www.therevisionbutton.co.uk/myrevisionnotes

In the weeks leading up to the exam it's important to make the most of your time. Make sure you've always got something on you to help you learn.

If you prefer pen and paper, you could write key facts onto small squares of paper, punch a hole in the top corner and then attach them to a key ring. This is small enough to fit into a pocket and you have the satisfaction of ripping off a fact each time you've learned it!

Method 5: Flashcards

On page 13 we give you some advice for creating revision cards on the key figures in the study of medicine. It would be a good idea to create similar cards for the key figures in your extension unit as well.

There are other ways you can use flashcards. Try writing dates on one set and facts on another, and try to match them up; or you could write two halves of a sentence, or discoveries and key figures. The possibilities are endless!

Exam technique

Understanding the exam

Your History GCSE is made up of three exams: **Development Study**, **Depth Study** and **Source Enquiry**. Each exam lasts for one hour and fifteen minutes, and is worth 25% of the total marks. Spread across all three papers are 10 marks for spelling, punctuation and grammar – so you will need to take care with these in your answers.

Unit 5HB01: Development Study

This book covers Medicine Through Time (pages 10–59).

You will need to answer five questions.

Question 1 is based around two sources and you will need to identify a change between the two. For example, you might be asked to look at two sources about female doctors, one from the nineteenth century and one from the twentieth century, and then identify the change in their status. This question is worth 8 marks, and to get full marks you will need to use your own knowledge to back up your inferences. Anybody could probably recognise a change, but knowing the background behind it is what demonstrates that you've studied this topic.

Question 2 is a knowledge recall question. You will need to have excellent subject knowledge and describe key features or facts about a particular time period, key figure or topic. This question is worth 6 marks, making it the least valuable question on the paper – so

don't spend too long on it. If you've done your revision properly you should be able to write plenty to answer this question in a short space of time.

> **Exam tip**
>
> Writing a good paragraph to explain an answer to something is as easy as **PEE**ing – Point, Example, Explain.
>
> Your point is a short answer to the question. You then back this up with lots of examples to demonstrate all the knowledge you have learned during your studies: this is the section that proves you have studied and revised, rather than just guessing. Finally you will link that knowledge to the question by explaining in a final sentence.
>
> **P**oint
>
> Passing my GCSE History exam will be very helpful in the future.
>
> **E**xample
>
> For example, it will help me to continue my studies next year.
>
> **E**xplain
>
> This will help me to get the job I want in the future.

Questions 3 is the second source question on the paper. In this question, you will be presented with a source and asked to judge how useful it is to a historian studying a certain topic. You should start doing this by considering its provenance – who wrote it, when and why – but in order to achieve more than half of the 8 marks available you will need to use some of your own knowledge to check its accuracy. This is why excellent subject knowledge is the bedrock of your success: if you read a source and it doesn't quite match what you know, you need to be confident enough in your own knowledge to be critical of that source.

Next, you will be asked to choose between **Questions 4 and 5**; both are worth 12 marks. You'll be given a picture or some bullet points to act as a stimulus, to jog your memory. You must also show some of your own knowledge in your answer, otherwise your maximum score will be 7 marks. Usually in this question you will be asked to assess change and continuity over time; for example, you might be asked how far hospital treatment has improved since 1750.

> ### Exam tip
> You don't have to use the bullet points but if you do, make sure you are using them to back up an explanation you have made rather than just copying them out – examiners hate that!

Finally, you will choose between **Questions 6 and 7**. You will be expected to build a balanced answer and reach an overall judgement. There are also 3 marks available for your spelling, punctuation and grammar, so take particular care here over key word spellings, capital letters and so on. You will get bullet points to jog your memory for these questions too, but, as before, you **must** bring in some of your own knowledge. This question is worth over a third of the marks on the paper, so consider answering it first – you don't need to answer the questions in a particular order when it comes to the exam.

Unit 5HB02: Depth Study

This book covers The American West (pages 68–105) and Nazi Germany (pages 106–128). You choose one only.

Like Unit 1, you will need to answer five questions, and **Question 1** is based on a source. You will need to look carefully at the source and make an inference from it. For example, you might be asked to look at a picture of a band of Plains Indians moving camp, and then make inferences about how their lifestyle was suited to the Plains. Again, it's important not to spend too long on this question – two good sentences are all you need.

You will have a choice for **Question 2**, and you will be asked to do some explaining again. It's really

easy to fall into the trap of writing down everything you know, so make sure you focus on the key words from the question to help you answer it clearly. Try taking a highlighter into the exam with you so that you can highlight the key words.

Next, you will choose either **Question 3** or **Question 4**, and like the Development paper, you will be given two bullet points to help jog your memory. You may use these bullets to get you started. Make sure you are **explaining** how they fit with the answer to the question and not just copying them out. You must also include your own knowledge.

Finally, you will choose either **Question 5** or **Question 6**. You should be able to answer either of them as long as you have done your revision properly! This question is in two parts and is worth half the marks for the paper. Part a will be a test of your knowledge and part b will require you to build a balanced answer, with an overall conclusion. Make sure you take careful note of any dates mentioned in the question and stick very closely to what you know within those dates – you won't get credit for anything from another time period. Use the bullet points to help you if you wish.

It is good practice to write a little plan, particularly for part b, which should be the longest answer on the exam. Draw a two-column chart and write bullet points on either side to help you build a balanced answer. One column will be agreeing with the statement or question, while the other will have points that disagree with it. This will help you to remember everything you want to write down and to present your answer in an organised and focused way.

> ### Exam tip
> When you're choosing between the two essay questions, if you have time, write a plan for BOTH part bs. Then you can make your choice based on which one you have more information for.

Unit 5HB03: Source Enquiry

This book covers The Transformation of Surgery c1845–c1918 (pages 60–67).

This exam is all about how well you handle sources. As well as having some subject knowledge, you will need to look at a number of written and picture sources and use them to answer five questions.

The key piece of advice here is – **DON'T PANIC!** The sources you see may not agree with what you thought you knew, but that doesn't always mean you are wrong! In fact, sometimes the examiner will throw in some sources that **deliberately** disagree with what you know, to see if you have done your revision. That's why it's important to revise carefully, and also to be confident in your own subject knowledge.

The paper will begin with some background information that you should read first, to give you an idea of the focus of the paper. Then read the sources through, underlining key words and taking note of the **provenance**. Once you have done this, start tackling the questions. Make sure you leave yourself plenty of time for **Question 5**, which is worth the most marks.

Question number	Marks	Key words	You need to...
1	6	What can you learn ...?	• Make an inference, or an educated guess, based on the source. • Use quotes from the source to back up your inference, or describe a specific part of it if it is a picture.
2	8	What was the purpose of this representation?	• Explain what the source is and why it was published – is it to publicise, to criticise, to educate ...? • Use your own knowledge to provide context.
3	10	Why ...?	• Use your own knowledge to answer this question, backed up by key facts from the source. • Use PEE paragraphs to help you explain.
4	10	How reliable are sources ... when studying ...?	• Use your own knowledge to judge how accurate the content of the sources is. • Use the source provenance to help you make a judgement about how reliable they are. • **DON'T** fall into the trap of talking about how useful they are. • Make sure you consider how reliable they are **for the enquiry specified**.
5	16 + 3	How far do you agree with the interpretation in Source ...?	• You need to evaluate a historical interpretation. Read the source specified and explain how far you agree with it. • Once you have done this, provide alternative interpretations, using the other sources and your own knowledge. • To access the highest marks you must use your own knowledge to provide that all-important context. • The extra 3 marks are for accurate spelling, punctuation and grammar. Write carefully and check your work to ensure you don't miss out on these marks.

1 An overview of medicine and treatment through time

Medicine and treatment is a Development Study. It is important to have a good understanding of all the content, then take a step back and make decisions about what has changed in medicine and treatment through time, and what has stayed the same. You should also have a basic understanding of the chronology of British history – that is, what happened and when. This will provide the context that will help you to explain **why** changes happened, and **why** some things stayed the same.

1.1 Creating a medicine and treatment timeline

Timelines are a really good way to help you to track changes and continuities in medicine. You can see on this version how quickly developments begin to occur after 1400! Making your own timeline will give you a better understanding of the chronology – the order in which key events and discoveries came along.

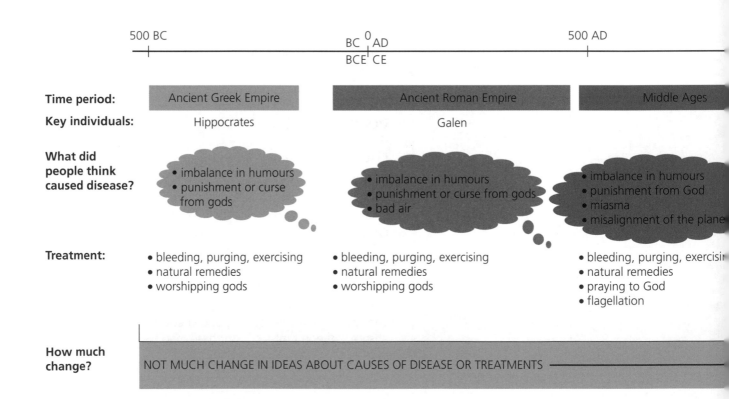

Create your own medicine and treatment timeline by copying the timeline below.

● Make yours as big as possible.

● As you revise the history of medicine and treatment, fill in the key events, individuals and discoveries.

● You could add your own illustrations to help you organise the detail.

● Use different colours or highlighters to show what relates to understanding the cause of disease, treatments, hospitals, training and public health.

● Then stick your timeline up somewhere you will see it frequently!

● You can download your blank timeline from www.therevisionbutton.co.uk/myrevisionnotes

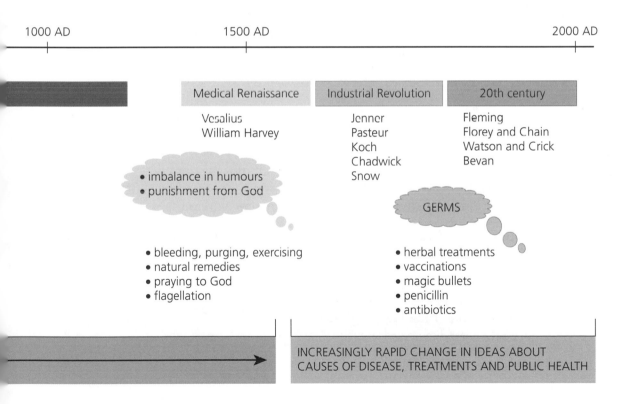

1000 AD   1500 AD   2000 AD

Medical Renaissance | Industrial Revolution | 20th century

Vesalius
William Harvey

Jenner
Pasteur
Koch
Chadwick
Snow

Fleming
Florey and Chain
Watson and Crick
Bevan

• imbalance in humours
• punishment from God

GERMS

• bleeding, purging, exercising
• natural remedies
• praying to God
• flagellation

• herbal treatments
• vaccinations
• magic bullets
• penicillin
• antibiotics

INCREASINGLY RAPID CHANGE IN IDEAS ABOUT
CAUSES OF DISEASE, TREATMENTS AND PUBLIC HEALTH

1.2 Factors affecting medicine and treatment

Many questions in your exam will ask you about 'factors'. These are things that:

- **helped to cause change** – for example, the factor **chance** led Fleming to discover penicillin when his dirty petri dishes started to grow mould
- **helped to prevent change** – for example, the factor **attitudes and beliefs** hindered knowledge of anatomy as religion banned dissection.

The main factors are shown in the diagram below, with an explanation of what they mean.

Government – the influence of those who governed Britain, their interest in the health of the population, and the laws and rules that were made about people's health.

Role of individuals – individuals made the effort or had the expertise to change things, mostly scientists and doctors who made great medical discoveries.

Chance – luck! As with everything, some medical developments were down to chance, or being in the right place at the right time.

FACTORS AFFECTING MEDICINE AND TREATMENT

Science and technology – new discoveries (science) and inventions (technology); not all of these were directly linked to medicine, but they still had an impact.

Attitudes and beliefs – religious attitudes and beliefs among the population, particularly with regard to new discoveries.

War – the impact not only of war and of being invaded when countries were fighting each other, but also of the increased travel and trade associated with it.

Revision task

Create a factor chart like the one below to fill in as you work through this revision guide. Draw it out on a large piece of paper, or create it as a file on a computer, so there is space to add lots of information. You can download a template from www.therevisionbutton.co.uk/myrevisionnotes.

Factor	Evidence of factor helping a development	Evidence of factor hindering a development
Government		
Role of individuals	Louis Pasteur came up with the germ theory, which helped people to understand what causes disease and infection.	
War		
Attitudes and beliefs		Religion banned dissection which hindered knowledge of anatomy.
Science and technology		
Chance	Alexander Fleming's petri dishes were contaminated with the penicillin spore by chance.	

As you work through the book, look out for these sticky notes:

(a)
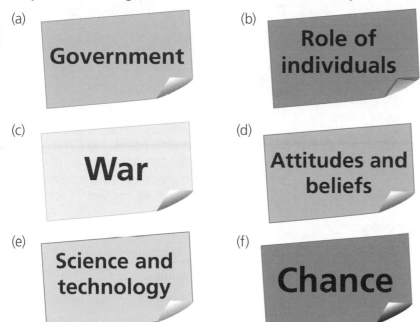
Government

(b)
Role of individuals

(c)
War

(d)
Attitudes and beliefs

(e)
Science and technology

(f)
Chance

When you see a sticky note that indicates a factor, add the relevant information from the text to your factor chart. Some revision tasks ask you to look particularly at factors. Add the work you complete for these tasks to your factor chart too. Medical megastars (see below) will give you lots of examples of the role of individuals.

When you have finished working through the book, look back at your completed factor chart. You should be able to recognise how the impact of these factors has changed over time, and make links between the factors and key time periods, for example the factor **science and technology** can be linked to industrialisation.

1.3 Medical megastars

Some individuals have so much influence on the history of medicine and treatment we could call them 'medical megastars', for example Galen, Vesalius and Pasteur. As you work through this book, create a revision card for each one. You should include key pieces of information:

↑ One example of a medical megastar is Vesalius

Name:

Period: (for example Ancient Rome, Renaissance)

Work:

Big idea:

Factors: (factors that helped or hindered them)

Short-term impact: (in their lifetime)

Long-term impact: (after their deaths)

↑ Another example is Harvey

2 The big picture of medicine from Roman Britain to c1350

The Romans invaded Britain in AD49 and brought their ideas about medicine with them. Although they left in the fifth century, some of their ideas, such as the teachings of Galen and the influence of Christianity, remained in Britain for a thousand years. The Church was very important throughout the Middle Ages and influenced every area of society.

Medicine in Roman Britain

These revision cards sum up the key things you need to know about Roman medicine.

Exam tip

These pages offer you a brief overview of the developments in medicine before c1350. Even if you are not doing the extension study for this time period, it will help you to have some background knowledge for your core content.

Revision task

Create a 'thinking Roman person' picture to help you summarise the key points of Roman ideas about medicine. Draw a stick person with thought bubbles coming out of his/her head. Write key words and draw pictures to summarise the information from the revision cards on this page.

I believe bad air can cause sickness.

The theory of the four humours

In Ancient Greece, a doctor and great thinker called Hippocrates developed his theory of the four humours.

- According to the theory of the four humours the body was made up of four humours: blood, phlegm, black bile and yellow bile. Too much or too little of any one of these humours (an **imbalance**) would cause on illness.
- The most common treatment for illness therefore was to **purge** whichever humour was in excess. This might take the form of bleeding, or causing a patient to vomit or clear their bowels.

Roman ideas about medicine

- The Romans took their ideas about medicine from the **Greeks**, for example the work of Hippocrates and the theory of the four humours (see above).
- The Romans believed in **gods** and viewed diseases as punishments from the gods. They built temples to ask their gods to cure them.
- They also believed **bad air** and smells could cause sickness, so built their settlements away from swamps. People believed in this theory until the time of the Renaissance.

The work of Galen

- Galen, a doctor to the Roman emperor, studied the work of Hippocrates.
- He followed Hippocrates' methods of **clinical observation** by closely observing his patients and recording their symptoms.
- He believed in Hippocrates' theory of the four humours (see above). However, Galen **adapted** it by suggesting new ways of balancing the humours, using opposites. For example, he prescribed hot chilli for an imbalance of phlegm.
- He also carried out dissections on animals and wrote about them in his books, which were studied right up until the time of the Renaissance.

Role of individuals –

Galen's work influenced medicine for more than 1500 years. This was both a help and a hindrance. Some of the treatments worked, but following Galen also prevented further experimentation.

The Romans and public health

The Romans saw a link between dirt and the spread of sickness. To prevent epidemics in their overcrowded towns and cities they developed public health schemes.

- **Public toilets** were provided, and **sewers** washed the waste away from the cities to nearby rivers.
- **Water pipes** were built from lead to carry clean water into towns for everyone to use. The towns had **public fountains** for drinking and **public baths** for washing.
- **Aqueducts** were built to transport water from rivers and lakes into towns and cities.

The collapse of the Roman Empire

When the Romans left Britain, war broke out between the countries that had been part of the Roman Empire. Things that the Romans had built were destroyed. This had an impact on medicine:

- **Public health** systems that the Romans had built were destroyed.
- **Libraries** full of medical books were dismantled.
- The invading tribes did not know how to read so they were not interested in **education** or the works of Galen.
- **War** was now the most important priority, and money was spent on armies rather than education and medicine.

The only powerful thing that survived the collapse of the Roman Empire was its religion – **the Christian Church.**

Medicine in Medieval Britain

These revision cards sum up the key things you need to know about medicine in the Middle Ages.

Revision task

Create a 'thinking medieval person' picture to help you summarise the key points of ideas about medicine in the Middle Ages. Draw a stick person with thought bubbles coming out of his/her head. Write key words and draw pictures to summarise the information from the revision cards on this page.

I believe illness and disease are punishments from God.

Ideas about the causes of disease in the Middle Ages

- People in the Middle Ages still believed in the work of Hippocrates and **the theory of the four humours,** as this was what the Church believed. They still treated people by purging and bleeding.
- They also believed that illness and disease were **punishments** from God. They had to **pray** to God for forgiveness.
- Like the Romans, they believed **bad air** and smells could cause sickness.

The influence of the Christian Church in the Middle Ages

- The Church taught that all illness was sent as a **punishment** from God. It was right for the person to suffer and cures should only come from God.
- The Church also supported Galen's and Hippocrates' ideas because they fitted the Christian idea that **one God created all humans**.
- The monasteries and convents had the best libraries and some of them provided **training for doctors.** They were taught the theory of the four humours and were not encouraged to prove Galen wrong.

Treatment in the Middle Ages

- Physicians, or doctors, probably had some medical training at a Church-run university.
- Doctors also studied **urine charts** and **astrology** to diagnose and treat illness. They had access to leechbooks which contained a mixture of Greek and Roman ideas about medicine as well as well-known herbal remedies.
- Doctors only treated the rich. Most illness was dealt with in the home by local **village healers** – usually women.
- Doctors did not attend childbirth. Women acted as **midwives** and attended births.
- **Wise women** provided herbal remedies and advice on curing illnesses and infections.
- **Hospitals** were places of rest and recuperation. They were not used for infectious or terminally ill patients. Hospitals were usually attached to monasteries or convents.

Public health and living conditions in the Middle Ages

Living conditions and health and hygiene were pretty bad, particularly in towns.

- City streets were covered in **rubbish** and animal and human waste.
- **Water** was often contaminated by other sources such as sewage and animal blood from butchers.
- Government **laws** to keep the streets clean were difficult to enforce.
- **Monasteries and convents** were generally healthier places as they had their own public health system with fresh water and toilets.

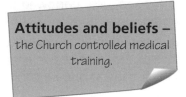

Attitudes and beliefs – the Church controlled medical training.

3 Medicine and public health from Roman Britain to c1350

3.1 The Romans and approaches to medicine

The Romans invaded Britain in AD43 and took control of the native population. Britain became part of the Roman Empire which ruled the country for the next four centuries. The influence of the Romans touched everything – building, structure of government, religious beliefs, medicine and, most importantly, public health. The Romans had some very big ideas about the importance of hygiene which they imposed on the people of Britain, as we will see on pages 19–21. They also brought with them new ideas about the causes and treatment of disease.

> **Key content**
> - Roman ideas about the causes of disease
> - The work of Galen
> - The influence of the Roman Empire

Roman ideas about the causes of disease

Revised

The Romans borrowed quite a lot of their understanding of medicine from the Greeks. They spread these ideas across their empire, which was the largest the world had ever seen. The Romans were very focused on what to do to improve health but did not spend time trying to come up with new explanations for what caused disease. They were happy to accept the Greek theory of the four humours, rather than spend time coming up with their own ideas.

- **The theory of the four humours** – The theory of the four humours was developed by Hippocrates in Ancient Greece. This theory suggested that the body was made up of four substances – blood, phlegm, yellow bile and black bile. An imbalance between these substances would cause an illness. Hippocrates therefore recommended bleeding or purging to get rid of excess humours as possible cures for diseases.

- **Punishments from the gods** – The Romans had strong religious beliefs. They regularly viewed diseases as punishments from the gods, or the results of curses. They built temples to their gods such as Asclepius, the god of healing, (also borrowed from the Greeks!) and worshipped and prayed to the gods for a cure.

- **Bad air** – They were also careful to build new settlements away from swamps, as they believed bad air and smells could cause sickness. This idea of bad air causing disease continued right up into the nineteenth century.

Exam tip

It is important to remember that the theory of the four humours was developed by Hippocrates (a Greek) and adopted by the Romans. You probably will not be asked to describe the theory in detail during the exam but you must focus on the **impact** the theory had on medicine – it was popular in Britain for more than a thousand years!

↑ **Bleeding**

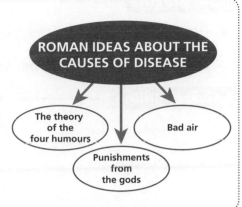

The work of Galen

Revised

Galen's career

Galen was a medical megastar of the second century AD. Born in Greece, he used his medical training to operate on wounds that gladiators received in combat before moving to Rome and becoming famous for his public dissections and medical lectures. He was eventually recruited to be the emperor's doctor, so his medical ideas became the most important in Rome. After all, who does not want to receive the same medical treatment as the emperor, the most important man in the empire?

The idea of opposites

Galen's big idea was built on Hippocrates' theory of the four humours (see page 16). Galen developed this theory with the idea of opposites, another way of introducing balance to the humours. Too much phlegm, for example, suggested that the illness was caused by **cold**, and therefore Galen used the 'opposite', that is **hot** ingredients such as chillies and peppers in his remedies.

Galen's dissections

Galen did dissections to learn about the inner workings of the human body. He had to make do with dissecting animals in Ancient Rome – mostly pigs and monkeys – but some of his conclusions about humans were correct. Galen wrote books about his dissections. Galen's dissections formed the basis for medical knowledge until the Renaissance.

Role of individuals –
Galen's theories provided the basis of medieval medical training.

Exam practice

2. How important was the influence of Hippocrates on Roman medicine? **(16 marks)**

Answers online

Exam tip

When tackling a big question like this, it is really important to write a balanced answer.

1. **On one hand:** Use the information on pages 16 and 17 to write a paragraph explaining the influence Hippocrates had on Roman medicine.
(Clue: he had a big influence on Galen.)

2. **On the other hand:** Write a paragraph to explain what other things influenced Roman medicine, such as religion and Galen's adaptations.

3. **Judgement:** Finally, weigh up your two paragraphs and write a conclusion, evaluating the impact Hippocrates had.

The influence of the Roman Empire

Revised

During the Roman Empire

- The Roman army was extremely well organised and offered excellent **medical training** for surgeons and doctors to treat its soldiers. Even though only the soldiers benefited directly, other citizens of the Roman Empire learned by example how to pick a good site for a settlement and provide clean water.

- The spread of violent entertainments such as gladiatorial combat meant that doctors became **skilled at treating wounds** and administering herbal remedies. Again, these doctors did not treat ordinary citizens – but it did mean that medical knowledge was exchanged and spread across Europe.

- The Romans were responsible for the spread of **Christianity** to Britain which remained after they had left.

After the Roman Empire

- Once the Romans had left Britain, a lot of **medical knowledge was lost** as their libraries were dismantled or destroyed and the army doctors returned to Rome. What remained was kept alive by the Church and its monasteries. The Christian Church was arguably the biggest legacy of the Roman Empire.

- The Church liked the work of Galen because **it fitted in with what the Bible taught** – that one God created all humans. Therefore the works of Galen continued to influence medicine in Britain right up to the Middle Ages.

Exam practice

3. How similar were approaches to medicine and treatment in Roman Britain and Anglo-Saxon Britain? **(12 marks)**

Answers online

Exam tip

This question requires you to explain similarities and differences in medicine between the Roman period and the early Middle Ages. You may want to bring in knowledge of public health in these two periods, as well as using information from the lists above.

3.2 Approaches to public health before 1350

The Romans may not have been particularly interested in coming up with new ideas about the causes of disease, but they certainly had an idea about how to prevent it. They recognised a link between dirt and the spread of sickness.

The city of Rome was hugely overcrowded and the authorities had to take steps to ensure its population kept clean and healthy, or they risked **epidemics**. They wanted to keep the public and the army healthy because they needed healthy soldiers, workers and merchants to keep the empire protected, fed and prosperous.

The Romans' big idea was public health. Government intervened to provide water supplies, sewer systems and public baths to improve the health of its population.

After the Romans left, however, many of their works fell into disrepair, and the standard of public health in Britain went down.

> ## Key content
> - How the Romans kept clean
> - The new technologies that the Romans used to improve public health
> - Public health in the early Middle Ages, up to 1350

How the Romans kept clean

Revised

The Romans encouraged their population to keep clean by making it as easy as possible! Even the smallest Roman town had a **public bath**, and people only had to pay a small amount to get in. A typical bathing experience might go something like this:

Meet up with your friends at the entrance to the baths.

Pop into the **yard** for some exercise – perhaps some wrestling, or weights.

Having worked up a sweat, move on to the **sauna** or **steam room**.

Call over a slave to **oil you** and then scrape the dirt from your body with a strigil.

Move on to the **warm** and **hot water pools** for a quick swim.

To finish, take a refreshing plunge in the frigidarium, or **cold pool**.

If this sounds like fun, it was meant to be. By making the baths a pleasant and cheap place to visit, the Romans encouraged their population to keep clean, which in turn led to better health.

The new technologies that the Romans used to improve public health

- **Aqueducts** – Roman aqueducts were marvellous feats of engineering. Often running for miles, they transported water from rivers and lakes into towns and cities where it was needed most. The aqueduct at Wroxeter could transport 2 million gallons of water a day – that is more than 20 gallons per second.

↑ Aqueduct

- **Water pipes** – Usually built from lead, these carried clean water into towns and distributed it among the population. Everybody was entitled to clean water. In Pompeii, for example, the water supply was distributed on three levels:
  - Firstly, the **public fountains** where people went to collect their fresh water were kept filled.
  - Secondly, the public baths were supplied.
  - Finally, any remaining water went to the private houses of the rich and the powerful.

  This meant that if there was a shortage of water, even the poorest were still able to access what there was.

↑ Public fountain

- **Public toilets** – These were provided, and people often went to meet for a chat as well as to relieve themselves. Sponges on sticks were provided instead of toilet paper.

↑ Public toilet

- **Sewers** – These carried waste away from public toilets and baths. The waste was washed away from the cities to nearby rivers.

↑ Sewer

Exam practice

1. Describe the key features of public health in Roman Britain. **(6 marks)**

Answers online

Exam tip

To help you answer this question, group the content on pages 19–20 into two sections:

1. bringing in clean water

2. taking away dirty water.

Then construct a paragraph for each section using the **PEE** method:

Point: A key feature of Roman public health was encouraging people to keep clean.

Example: They did this by ...

Explain: This helped to improve public health by ...

Public health in the early Middle Ages, up to 1350

Revised ☐

As mentioned in Chapter 2, after the Romans left Britain in the fifth century AD, a lot of their works fell into disrepair. The native population did not have the training or technology to maintain the aqueducts and public baths, and the rulers of individual kingdoms did not see the point in spending the money. By 1350, the public health picture was rather mixed.

Positive	Negative
● The rich had high standards of cleanliness, and many had a **privy** (toilet) that was separate from living quarters. ● **Lead pipes** supplied water to the houses of merchants and local dignitaries. ● The standard of **hygiene in monasteries and convents** was usually quite high. Fresh water was piped in and human waste disposed of in running water. ● Some town councils provided fresh water and public baths, known as **stewes**, to help the population keep clean and healthy.	● Lead pipes for water were usually only laid if they could be privately funded. They were **leaky** and gave the water a **bad taste**. ● Water was often **contaminated** by other sources and was not healthy as a drink. ● Town streets were strewn with **rubbish** and **human and animal waste**. This attracted a lot of rats. ● The government sometimes passed laws requiring people to keep the streets clean – especially in times when disease was common – but these were **difficult to enforce**. ● In most places there was **no public provision** of clean water.

Exam practice

2. 'After the Romans left Britain the progress they had made in public health did not continue.' Do you agree? Explain your answer. **(16 marks)**

Answers online

Government – they did not think it was their job to improve public health.

Exam tip

When tackling this question, use the table above to help you evaluate the progress made in public health after the Romans left Britain.

1. Highlight the things that show public health **progressed**, or improved, in one colour.

2. Use another colour to highlight the things that show public health **stayed the same**, or went backwards (**regression**).

3. Make sure you include a **conclusion**, explaining your overall answer to the question.

Key term

Regression – the opposite of progression. Regression is when things get worse not better.

3.3 The impact of religion

The Church played such a major role in life in the early Middle Ages that it affected almost everything, medicine included! It both helped and hindered medicine. We know the Church stopped doctors from experimenting and dissecting, which kept medical knowledge at a standstill for a number of centuries. However, the Church promoted real medical learning in facilities that today we would call universities. It also played a large part in caring for sick people who did not have family members to look after them.

Key content

- The impact of religion on the development of medical knowledge
- The role of the Church in training doctors
- What the Church taught about the causes of disease
- The importance of the Church in caring for the sick

Attitudes and beliefs – the Church banned dissection, but set up medical schools.

The impact of religion on the development of medical knowledge

Revised

- The Church remained the only **constant authority** in British history from the Romans to the Middle Ages. Missionaries came to Britain after the Romans had gone to keep God's church alive. They maintained libraries preserving medical knowledge.
- Since the Church had the monopoly on medical treatment and training (apart from local village healers), it was able to choose which books were copied and distributed, and what medical knowledge was shared. **Therefore, the works of Galen appeared everywhere.**

- Sick people were encouraged to **pray** to various saints for healing. Each ailment had its own saint – St Blaise was the saint of sore throats, for example.
- The Church did share some of its power with **the king** by anointing him with holy oil when he was crowned. It was believed that this gave him healing powers. Kings were supposed to be particularly good at healing scrofula, a form of tuberculosis, which they did by laying their hands on sufferers. This belief started in the eleventh century and continued for many centuries.

> **Key term**
>
> **Monopoly** – one organisation or person controls every aspect of a trade or profession.

The role of the Church in training doctors

Revised

Medical literature

- During the Middle Ages, the majority of doctors **trained by reading books**. Since the best libraries were in monasteries and convents, trainee doctors spent a lot of time there.
- Some of these religious institutions developed into **universities**, which were controlled by the Church.
- By the twelfth century it was difficult to practise as a doctor without studying for a few years. This meant the Church maintained its control over the medical profession until the **Reformation**.

> **Key term**
>
> **Reformation** – when the Reformation happened in Britain, Henry VIII founded the Church of England, destroying monasteries and other Catholic institutions in the process.

Teaching Galen

The Church loved Galen so much that it would not let anybody criticise him or try to prove his ideas wrong. Therefore doctors were thoroughly trained in the theory of the four humours.

↑ Galen

What the Church taught about the causes of disease

Revised

Natural explanations

- Galen had said that disease was caused by an imbalance in humours, and so that is what the Church said too. Popular remedies for disease were bleeding via cuts or leeches, purging and treating with opposites. Pus was to be encouraged – it was a 'sign of healing'.

Revision task

Compare Roman beliefs about causes of disease with what the Church taught in the Middle Ages. Use the information from these pages and from pages 16–20 to help you complete the table below.

Roman beliefs about causes of disease	What the Church taught about causes of disease in the Middle Ages
Imbalance in the four humours	Imbalance in the four humours

When you have finished your table, highlight all the beliefs that appear in both columns.

Supernatural explanations

- There was a strong belief, promoted by the Church, that illness and disease were caused by **sin**. This meant that prayer was the easiest cure; and, of course, you could go along to church and pay someone to pray for you. Sick people also went on pilgrimages to saints' shrines to make offerings.
- This belief also encouraged people to live according to the rules of the Church day-to-day, and to **attend church** regularly to help them avoid getting ill in the first place.
- **Astrology** was also used in the treatment of the sick. The position of the moon, for example, was said to be particularly important when bleeding a patient.

The importance of the Church in caring for the sick

Revised

Over a thousand hospitals were set up in Britain during the Middle Ages which were all run by monks or nuns. Their main job was to pray for the soul of the sick person – **remember that they thought God might have sent the disease in the first place**.

Unfortunately, because God knew best, the monks and nuns did not think it was their job to actually **cure** the patients – only to look after them until God decided what to do with them. For this reason, very few hospitals actually employed a doctor.

A lot of hospitals refused to admit infectious or incurable patients because there was no medical professional to look after them. So **British hospitals in the Middle Ages were very different to the hospitals we have today** – and this was as a direct result of the Church's teachings on the causes of disease.

However, life was hard in the Middle Ages and the chance to rest in a warm, clean, comfortable environment and eat good food for a few days probably would have been enough to cure some of the patients that came through the doors.

Exam practice

1. How far did ideas about the cause of disease change from the Roman period to the end of the Middle Ages? **(16 marks)**

Answers online

Exam tip

For this question, use the table you completed for the revision task to help you build your two-sided balanced answer to the question.

3.4 The impact of government and war

Alongside the Church, the government was able to have a lot of influence on the health of its citizens. This influence could be positive, such as the Roman government's promotion of public health. It could also be negative, such as medieval governments not feeling it was their job to get involved in matters of health.

War also had an effect on the development of medicine and treatment. Army surgeons got practice in treating wounds and the need for a healthy army led to improvements in water supplies and sanitation in the Roman Empire.

> **Government –** populations didn't value public health if their rulers didn't.

> **War –** war led to new ideas, but also a loss of knowledge.

Key content

- The impact of government
- The impact of war

The impact of government

Revised

The government of Ancient Rome

- The emperor and his government funded **public works** to promote good public health. They thought healthy citizens were less likely to rebel and healthy workers and merchants were important for a prosperous empire.
- Galen was the emperor's doctor, and he was encouraged to **publish** his texts. He taught many other doctors.

The government of the early Middle Ages

- Kings and their advisers had little interest in medicine. They were more interested in defending their kingdoms, and did not recognise that healthy subjects would help with this. And anyway, the Church controlled most aspects of medicine.
- This lack of interest probably had a negative effect on public health. If the king did not care about it, why should anybody else?

The impact of war

Revised

War in Ancient Rome

War brought the Romans to Britain. They brought with them new medical knowledge that stayed for over 1500 years. They also brought with them new standards of cleanliness and a new emphasis on hygiene.

However, war also led to the Romans leaving Britain. Their libraries and public works fell into decay, and a lot of medical knowledge was lost. It is easy to understand why medicine went backwards after they left.

War in the early Middle Ages

In the Middle Ages, war had some positive effects, for example there were soldiers who travelled to the Middle East to fight in the Crusades and brought medical knowledge back with them.

Exam practice

1. To what extent did medicine and public health change between the Roman withdrawal from Britain and c1350? **(16 marks)**

Answers online

Exam tip

Use the information on pages 21–24 to help you build a balanced answer. Your two sides will be 'lots of change' and 'hardly any change'. Don't forget to write an overall conclusion, explaining how much you think things changed.

4 Medicine and treatment c1350–c1750

4.1 Medicine at the time of the Black Death

The **Black Death** arrived in Britain towards the end of the fourteenth century and remained a regular scourge for several centuries, killing nearly half the population. People had no idea what caused it, or how best to treat it; they stuck to the old remedies, such as bleeding or herbal remedies, or they turned to prayer. The hospitals at the time knew better than to admit sufferers of the Black Death, most of whom were going to die anyway. Most sufferers were cared for at home by women and tended to by local healers.

Key content

- Ideas about medicine and treatment in 1350
- The Black Death and how it was treated
- The types of health care available c1350–c1750

Ideas about medicine and treatment in 1350 — Revised

Since the fall of the Roman Empire in the fifth century, a lot of medical knowledge had been lost in Britain and doctors now relied on Roman and Greek medical books preserved by the Arabs. Additionally, the great strides in public health made by the Romans, with their running water and habit of regular bathing, were completely forgotten.

- Doctors diagnosed their patients by looking at their urine and using **astrology** – working out the positions of the planets and the moon.
- The most common treatment was **bleeding**. Doctors were taught the **theory of the four humours** (see page 16) at medical school and they believed that it was vital to keep the humours in balance.
- **Herbal remedies** were popular and treatment often started at home.
- Most villages had a healer, usually a **wise woman**, who could mix up something for everyday illnesses.

Key terms

Astrology – the study of the planets and how they might influence the lives of people.

Bleeding – the practice of cutting a patient and draining away some blood. This might be done with a knife and a bleeding cup, or with leeches. Monastery records show that monks were bled regularly; the blood was often kept and used as a fertiliser in the fields.

The Black Death and how it was treated — Revised

- The Black Death was probably **bubonic plague**.
- Bubonic plague was spread by fleas carried on rats, which travelled on trading ships. This meant the disease **quickly spread around Europe**, with ports being the first affected.
- The disease began like a **fever**, with chills and shivering.
- Then swellings, called **buboes**, appeared in the groin and armpits, followed by blisters all over the body.
- The victim's temperature soared, causing a high **fever**, unconsciousness and then death.
- **Pneumonic plague** often went hand in hand with bubonic plague. This caused the victim to cough up blood and struggle to breathe.

People in the Middle Ages did not know what actually caused the Black Death and therefore did not know how to cure it. But they did have plenty of ideas for explanations and treatments.

Suggested explanations	Suggested treatments
Bad air	Those who believed bad air was to blame would burn barrels of tar to drive away the 'bad' air.
God had sent the plague as a punishment	Flagellants would walk through towns beating themselves to show God how sorry they were. Even for those who did not think this was necessary, regular prayer and church attendance was still a must.
Jews poisoning the wells	In some parts of Europe, Jewish populations were massacred.
An imbalance in the four humours	Bleeding or purging.
An unlucky alignment of the planets	No solution.

Large numbers of people died from the Black Death. In some places there weren't enough people left alive to bury the bodies of plague victims. Whole villages were deserted.

Exam practice

1. Why was the Black Death such a problem in Britain from c1350 onwards? **(12 marks)**

Answers online

Exam tip

The simple answer to this question is that people were unable to cure the Black Death, or to stop it from spreading. Use the chart and information above to help you find examples for each of these two points. Then explain why they led to the Black Death being such a problem.

The types of health care available c1350–c1750

Revised

The majority of people who needed medical attention in the Middle Ages were cared for by a female family member. Treatment went on in the home (which is another reason why the plague spread so quickly among families) and was usually based around herbal remedies. These might have been mixed by an apothecary or a quack, or by the local wise woman. For those who did not have anyone to care for them, hospitals were the only other option.

Hospitals in 1350

- They were run by **monks and/ or nuns** who believed that God might have sent the illness in the first place. Therefore medical care was mainly focused on praying for the souls of the patients.
- There were no medical professionals to look after the ill, so hospitals **did not admit** infectious or incurable patients.
- They were almost exclusively run as **care homes** for the elderly.

Hospitals between 1350 and 1750

The dissolution of the monasteries by Henry VIII in the middle of this time period (1500s) had a huge impact on the way hospitals were run because the monasteries had provided hospital care. Instead, local people, charities and town councils paid for hospitals to be opened. By 1750 there had been major changes.

Hospitals by 1750

- They were run by **trained physicians** and by nurses who did not have medical training.
- Some hospitals, particularly in the biggest cities, now **admitted infectious patients**.
- Herbal remedies and minor surgery were common, although **prayer** still featured heavily.

4.2 Ideas about the causes of disease: the influence of the past

Universities started to appear in the twelfth century. They trained doctors using the 1000-year-old works of Galen and Hippocrates. These were widely used in the Islamic world and reached Europe thanks to increased travel and trade.

Key content

- The influence of Galen

The influence of Galen

Revised ☐

You were introduced to medical megastar Galen on page 17. By 1350, his ideas were over 1000 years old, but they were still being followed by doctors.

- The Church liked Galen because he taught that all the parts of the body **fitted together** into a well-designed whole. This fitted in with what the Bible taught about man being made in God's image.
- The Church also supported the **theory of the four humours**. Bleeding was a very common treatment in monasteries.
- Medical training was **controlled** by the Church. Therefore all trainee **physicians** learned about Galen.
- The Church controlled the **libraries**. It chose what to translate and copy, so it picked Galen's books.
- The Church did not allow human **dissection**. Medical students had to go on what Galen taught because they were not able to discover anything different for themselves.

Revision task

Find the revision card you started for Galen (see page 17). Add some more notes under 'long-term impact', using the information here.

Key term

Physicians – doctors of medicine who trained at university.

Exam practice

1. How useful is Source A to a historian who is studying ideas about medicine c1350 to c1750? Use the source and your own knowledge to explain your answer. **(8 marks)**

Answers online

Exam tip

To answer this question well you need to consider what this source is useful *for*. Clearly it can give you information about the four humours, and if you look carefully you will see the signs of the zodiac, which give you a hint about other medical ideas at this time. However, there are lots of beliefs about medicine that this source does not show – and this is where your own knowledge comes in. Make sure you write about what the source shows, and what it does not show.

Exam tip

Don't forget to consider the reliability of the source. Does it fit with what you already know about this time period? Does it come from a publication that is likely to be trustworthy?

Source A: An illustration of the four humours taken from *Quinta Essentia*, a medical encyclopedia written in the sixteenth century

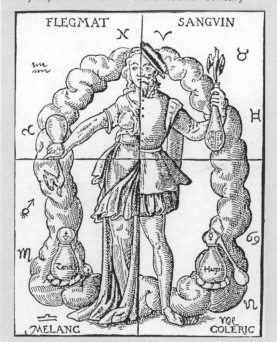

4.3 The impact of the Renaissance on medicine and medical training

The word 'renaissance' literally means 'rebirth'. In history, the Renaissance period is when people believed that the love of knowledge had been 're-born'. They believed that this would lead to great progress. From the start of the fifteenth century, new ideas and theories swept across Europe. This had a big impact on every area of learning. Ancient Greek and Roman writings became popular again, and as a result so did the Greek and Roman attitudes of observation, enquiry and investigation. People began to challenge ideas and this led to new developments in medicine.

Key content

- The Renaissance – new knowledge, technology and ideas
- The impact of the Renaissance on medical training
- The impact of the Royal Society on medicine

The Renaissance – new knowledge, technology and ideas

Revised

- **Art** – Artists began to draw and sculpt from life, which led to more accurate depictions of the human body. Leonardo da Vinci, for example, carried out human dissections and produced detailed drawings of the inside of the human body. Although these were never published, there were many other artists who shared their work with physicians. The physicians used these to gain knowledge and improve their own practice.

- **Printing** – The invention of the printing press was new technology that had a huge impact on the development of medicine. It was now possible to produce books cheaply and quickly. Knowledge and ideas could be shared across Europe more easily. More people learned to read because there were more books available to read. This meant there was a lot more thinking going on too.

- **Exploration** – Adventurous types like Columbus sailed around the world, bringing back with them interesting new plants like potatoes, tobacco and tomatoes. New sea routes were established with Asia and Africa, strengthening the connection between these continents and Europe.

- **New machinery** – The invention of the pump helped to give people ideas about how the body worked. The pump was a big inspiration to Harvey when he started thinking about the circulation of the blood round the body (see page 31). New techniques in glass making were developed, which eventually led to the invention of the microscope.

Science and technology – new ideas in lots of different disciplines impacted medicine.

Exam practice

1. Why were art and printing so important in improving medical understanding during the Renaissance?
   (12 marks)

Answers online

Revision task

Create a concept map like this to show all the new developments during the Renaissance. Add notes to explain how each new development affected medicine.

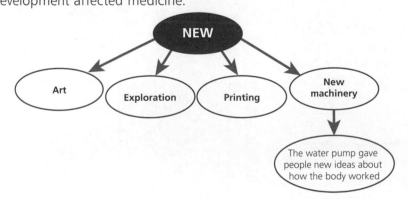

NEW

Art   Exploration   Printing   New machinery

The water pump gave people new ideas about how the body worked

Exam tip

Use the information from your concept map to help you answer this question. Remember to use the **PEE** method (see page 7): the information from your concept map will form the **E**xamples in your answer.

The impact of the Renaissance on medical training

Revised

- The Renaissance was an age of **new discoveries** and this encouraged medical students to **experiment**. Trail-blazers like Vesalius and Paracelsus, another famous Renaissance doctor and medical professor, set examples for their students.
- The Church no longer controlled medical training because it had become less powerful after the Reformation. This meant there was more scope for **challenging the old ideas** and less emphasis on the supernatural.
- Students were encouraged to carry out **practical training** in hospitals, where they would examine patients and keep a record of their symptoms.
- **Dissection** was now common, although bodies were in short supply. This was very different from medical training before the Renaissance, when students had relied on books to tell them everything they needed to know.

The impact of the Royal Society on medicine

Revised

The Renaissance led to other big changes, including the Scientific Revolution, which began towards the end of the sixteenth century. It was triggered by the ideas of Copernicus, who came up with the idea that the Earth moved around the Sun, and the ideas of Vesalius (see page 30). Logic, reasoning and experimentation now became the focus of scientific research.

This new fashion for scientific research led to the founding of the Royal Society in London, which began meeting in 1645. Later, it received a royal charter from King Charles II, who became its patron. The motto of the members was *Nullis in verba*, which means 'Take nobody's word for it' – and they didn't! The Royal Society was committed to the idea of experimentation and gave money to scientists who were willing to try new things. It also sponsored translations of foreign books about experiments.

By championing enquiry and experimentation, the Royal Society helped to drive forward medical research in Britain. Young doctors and anatomists went to the Royal Society for money, either to carry out their research or for help publishing it.

Revision task

Write an information leaflet for somebody considering joining the Royal Society. Explain:

- why it was set up
- what its goals are
- why it is an important institution. (Hint: what sort of things did it do that nobody else did?)

4.4 Medical megastars: Vesalius and Harvey

Vesalius and Harvey are our next two medical megastars. Although they were separated by nearly a century, they were both instrumental in proving that Galen had not always been right.

Vesalius and the human body

Revised

There were lots of professors of surgery by the sixteenth century, of which Vesalius was just one. Vesalius was born in 1514 in Brussels. He moved to Padua in Italy, where he was a Professor of Surgery. The thing that set him apart from his fellow surgeons was his enquiring mind, and his particular interest was the human body. He even stole a criminal's corpse when he was a child because he wanted to learn more about anatomy!

The printing press

At Padua University, he was able to carry out his own dissections and find artists who were willing to make detailed drawings of the human body. He published these drawings, together with his findings, in a book called *The Fabric of the Human Body* (1543) to help his students better understand human anatomy. This book became the first modern anatomical textbook. Thousands of copies were printed and used all over Europe. This helped to improve the training of doctors.

Vesalius also insisted his medical students carry out detailed observations of their work, and sometimes his as well, to ensure no mistakes were made. His work inspired the next generation to find out for themselves rather than believing what they were taught.

↑ **An illustration from Vesalius' book**

Science and technology – printing meant new ideas could be spread more quickly.

How Vesalius disagreed with Galen

Revised

It is not surprising that Vesalius disagreed with Galen because Galen had been dissecting animals, whereas Vesalius was dissecting real human bodies (including his father's and his sister's!). The table below shows some of Galen's ideas, and how Vesalius disagreed with them.

Role of individuals – Renaissance thinkers paved the way for eighteenth- and nineteenth-century scientists.

Galen	Vesalius
The human lower jawbone is made up of two pieces, like an animal lower jawbone.	Dissections of humans show that the human lower jawbone is one piece.
Blood moves from one side of the heart to the other through holes in the middle piece.	This is definitely wrong – there are no holes in the septum. Further research is needed to find out how it really moves.
The breastbone is made up of seven parts.	The breastbone is made up of three parts.
The liver has five lobes.	The liver has no lobes – it is just one big liver.

Revision task

On the illustration above from Vesalius' book, label the parts of the body that Vesalius proved Galen wrong about.

Exam practice

1. Why was Vesalius able to prove Galen wrong in the sixteenth century? *(12 marks)*

Answers online

Key term

Context – the set of facts or circumstances that surround a particular event.

Exam tip

When you are considering the reasons why Vesalius was able to prove Galen wrong, **how** he did it will only form part of your answer. You also need to explain **why** Vesalius was able to carry out his research during this particular time period. This is called context, and here it is all to do with other factors.

The main factor is new technology because the printing press was very helpful in spreading Vesalius' ideas. Look back at the factors in the chart on page 12 to help you decide if any others were important.

Harvey's 'big idea' – the circulation of the blood

Revised ☐

A century after Vesalius published his book, a lot of people still believed Galen's ideas about blood. Galen said that new blood was produced by the liver and burned up in the body. He also said that blood passed from one side of the heart to the other through invisible holes. William Harvey was born in 1578 in Kent and became a lecturer in anatomy in London. He did a lot of research on the heart and published his own book on the circulation of blood in 1628.

- Harvey claimed that the heart acted as a **pump**, pushing blood around the body.
- He carried out simple experiments to show that **arteries** carried blood away from the heart and **veins** carried the blood back.
- He discovered that **valves** in veins forced the blood to move in a one way system.
- He did an experiment to calculate that the amount of blood going into arteries each hour was three times the weight of a man.
- This proved that Galen's idea that the blood was produced by the liver and then used as it travelled around the body was **wrong**. There would simply be too much blood for it all to be absorbed and so it had to be the *same* blood that was being pumped around the body.
- Harvey theorised that **tiny blood vessels** connected veins and arteries, and fed the whole body with blood. He was right, though he did not have the technology to be able to see these vessels.

↑ Harvey

Revision task

Create your medical megastars revision cards for Vesalius and Harvey (see page 13). You should add key pieces of information, including the short-term and long-term impact of their discoveries.

Although Vesalius and Harvey can both be considered medical megastars due to the importance of their discoveries, don't forget to think about the short-term impact as well. In the short term, their ideas did not lead to many changes because they did not actually make a difference to the way that people were treated. Also, doctors at the time were reluctant to admit that Galen had been wrong, and it took many years to change their minds.

Exam practice

2. The bullets below show two key figures from the medical renaissance. Choose one and describe the key features of their medical discoveries.
   - Andre Vesalius
   - William Harvey *(6 marks)*

Answers online

Exam tip

This question is all about what you can remember and is worth the least amount of marks on the paper. Make sure you revise thoroughly so that you have the facts at your fingertips, and then it shouldn't take you too long to answer.

4.5 Public health c1350–c1750

We have already seen that, after the Romans left, their public health schemes were left to fall into disrepair and public health was no longer on the agenda for the government. This meant that towns were unhealthy places – but there were not many of them and not many people lived there. However, this situation began to change between 1350 and 1750. There were also regular outbreaks of plague, which presented a big public health problem for the authorities.

Key content

- Health problems in towns in the Middle Ages
- Actions taken by governments in the Middle Ages

Health problems in towns in the Middle Ages

Revised

If you have ever been to a festival, you know that if 100,000 people get together for a weekend it can get very messy. The ground gets muddy. Toilets overflow. Everyone gets dirty. Some people get food poisoning. Medieval towns contained far fewer people than a modern festival but the same principles applied.

However it's not all bad!

Don't slip into the stereotype that the Middle Ages were all filth and squalor. Nobles took baths, monasteries had flush latrines and lavers (wash rooms). There were dozens of stewes (public bath houses).

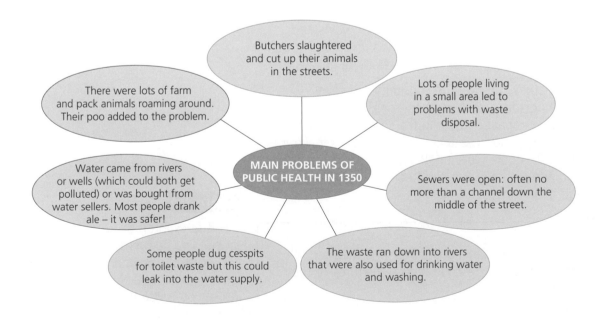

Butchers slaughtered and cut up their animals in the streets.

There were lots of farm and pack animals roaming around. Their poo added to the problem.

Lots of people living in a small area led to problems with waste disposal.

MAIN PROBLEMS OF PUBLIC HEALTH IN 1350

Water came from rivers or wells (which could both get polluted) or was bought from water sellers. Most people drank ale – it was safer!

Sewers were open: often no more than a channel down the middle of the street.

Some people dug cesspits for toilet waste but this could leak into the water supply.

The waste ran down into rivers that were also used for drinking water and washing.

Actions taken by governments in the Middle Ages

- Some English kings tried to make laws to improve conditions in towns so that waste was not emptied into the streets and cesspits were emptied regularly (for example, the Law of 1388).

- However, on the whole, the King and central government weren't very interested in making laws about public health. This was left to the town councils. The towns had the problem, let them deal with it themselves!

- No-one wanted to live in a smelly dirty place so towns had laws that citizens had to keep the streets clean and dispose of their rubbish properly, but they didn't have the clout or the money to make sure this was done.

- There were some **rakers** employed by the local authorities to keep the streets clean, but there were not enough of them.

- There was no organised rubbish collection and people had to empty their own cesspits, or pay somebody (known as a **gongfermer**) to do it for them.

- During the sixteenth and seventeenth centuries they even built a network of wooden pipes in London to provide water, but these were unreliable and easily damaged.

Key terms

Rakers – people employed by the local authorities to keep the streets clean.

Quarantine – separating sick people from healthy people to prevent disease spreading.

And during an epidemic they did a lot more

There were regular outbreaks of diseases such as plague. When this happened in London the authorities took some sensible actions; for example, during the Great Plague they:

- burned dirty clothes
- appointed extra rakers to collect rubbish
- killed dogs and cats
- isolated victims (**quarantine**), appointed searchers to examine for signs of sick people to quarantine and appointed Constables to shut up infected houses
- fired guns into the sky to break up the bad air.

Sometimes the plague led to so many deaths that mass pits had to be dug to bury all the bodies quickly, before they caused more disease.

However, in spite of all this, on balance the government did very little for public health between 1350 and 1750.

- Central government did not think it was their job. Local government lacked **money**, **understanding, desire** and **power**.

- In an epidemic they might take action but they did not know what caused disease, so these measures were not effective. And, once the epidemic had gone, things went back to how they had been. Little was learnt about how to prevent it coming back.

We could sum it up like this: between 1350 and 1750, governments simply **reacted** to problems as they occurred.

Exam practice

1. Why did people living in towns have problems accessing fresh water in the period 1350–1750?

(12 marks)

Answers online

5 Medicine and treatment c1750–c1900

5.1 Medical megastars: Jenner and vaccination

In the eighteenth century, smallpox was a **scourge** on the population. Outbreaks every few years killed many and left many others with terrible scarring. Families suffering from smallpox were isolated from their communities and were unable to work, which caused economic hardship. Enter Jenner. At the end of the eighteenth century he developed the first vaccination, which was used to tackle the smallpox scourge in Britain.

> **Role of individuals –** the first vaccination showed disease prevention was possible.

Key content

- Why Jenner tried to prevent smallpox
- How Jenner developed vaccination
- What people thought of vaccination

Key term

Scourge – a cause of disease or disaster.

Why Jenner tried to prevent smallpox

Revised

Previous research

- People had been trying to tackle smallpox for a long time. The Chinese had had some success by deliberately exposing people to a mild form of smallpox; this, they had discovered, prevented more severe attacks later. This was known as **inoculation**.
- Lady Mary Wortley Montagu, the wife of the British Ambassador to Turkey, came across inoculation in Turkey and was very taken with it. She was an influential woman who had many doctor friends, and she had her children inoculated in 1721.
- When inoculation reached Britain, it was used in Maidstone during a 1766 epidemic with some success.

Observation

Jenner was a rural doctor who was trained in methods of scientific experimentation. He was taught by John Hunter, a famous surgeon, who encouraged his students to observe carefully and carry out their own experiments. Jenner noticed that people who had had cowpox (a mild disease, like chickenpox) did not catch smallpox. Jenner made a connection between inoculation and the fact that those who had had cowpox did not catch smallpox. So, in 1796, he decided to carry out an experiment.

How Jenner developed vaccination

Revised

1 He took pus from the sores of a cowpox sufferer.
2 He rubbed pus into some cuts on the arm of a young boy.
3 He treated the young boy for cowpox.
4 Six weeks later, he attempted to infect the same boy with smallpox, but the boy did not catch it.
5 He repeated this experiment 23 times to be certain, with the same outcome each time.

Revision task

Draw a five-frame storyboard of the invention of vaccination. Label the key features of each stage in Jenner's experiment.

Vaccination had been born! Jenner is a good example of the way medical training had improved considerably by the end of the eighteenth century.

Key term

Vaccination – the name Jenner gave to his method. It comes from *vacca*, the Latin word for cow.

Source A: 'The Cow-Pock – or – the Wonderful Effects of the New Inoculation!' by James Gillray

The COW-POCK — or — the Wonderful Effects of the New Inoculation! _Vide.. the Publications of ye Anti-Vaccine Society._

Revision task

Look at Source A carefully. What is going on? Do you think the artist thought vaccination was a good thing? Create two lists of things you can see in Source A under the headings:

● Vaccination is good

● Vaccination is bad.

To begin with, Jenner met resistance.

● The Royal Society (see page 29) refused to publish his work, so he had to raise the money to publish it himself.

● Jenner was not able to explain how his vaccination worked. This made people suspicious.

● Doctors who had been making lots of money from inoculations were not keen to provide free vaccinations on government grants.

● Vaccination was not always successful thanks to careless doctors using infected needles and mixing up their cowpox and smallpox samples.

On the other hand the British government was supportive of Jenner's ideas, and abroad people were a bit more trusting:

● Napoleon had his whole army vaccinated in 1805.

● The American President Thomas Jefferson championed his ideas.

● Jenner's book was translated into Arabic and Turkish and sold across Asia.

It just took a bit more time in Britain, where the population remained largely sceptical and suspicious even after the government made the vaccine compulsory in 1852, but it wasn't widely enforced.

Luckily, Jenner's perseverance and that of his supporters paid off. In 1872 the British government started enforcing the compulsory vaccine, which led to a massive drop in the number of cases. By 1980, the disease had been eradicated worldwide.

In the long term, Jenner's vaccination was amazingly successful.

Revision task

Create a revision card for Jenner (see page 13). When you are explaining the impact of Jenner's work, it is important to look at it in both the short term and the long term. Like many medical megastars, Jenner had to wait a while before his work got the credit it deserved.

Source B: From BBC news, reporting on a shortage of flu vaccines in January 2011

'GPs ran out of seasonal flu jabs earlier this month, forcing ministers to turn to stockpiles of the old swine flu vaccine – which does not offer protection against all the strains of flu circulating this winter. Most vaccines, including the entire childhood immunisation programme, are ordered by the Department of Health for the whole of the UK.'

Exam practice

1. What do Sources A and B show about changes in attitudes towards vaccination? **(8 marks)**

Answers online

5.2 Medical megastars: Pasteur and Koch

The 1860s was a massive turning point in medicine: for the first time it was proved that germs caused disease. People had known about the link between dirt and disease for centuries, but nobody knew exactly why dirt caused disease, and often blamed bad air or miasma. However, thanks to a new, more powerful microscope and some heavy investment from the brewing industry, germ theory was finally developed. Louis Pasteur in France and Robert Koch in Germany were both instrumental in the development of our understanding of germs.

Role of individuals –
Pasteur discovered germs and Koch began to study them.

Key term

Miasma – bad air, or smells from rubbish and human waste rotting in the streets, which were thought to cause disease.

Key content

- The impact of germ theory
- The importance of research teams in the development of germ theory and the discovery of the first microbes

The impact of germ theory

Revised

The development of germ theory

Louis Pasteur was a chemist who worked in France. In the 1850s, he was asked by wine producers to find out why their alcohol went sour.

- Using a new microscope, he discovered micro-organisms were making the alcohol go sour. He called these **germs**.
- He discovered that if any liquid was heated, the germs were killed. This process was called **pasteurisation**.
- Pasteur went on to prove that these germs caused disease in animals and humans. He published his germ theory of disease in 1861. However, he was a scientist, not a doctor, and it was left to others to pick up where he left off.

Koch's study of bacteria

Robert Koch was a German doctor who studied Pasteur's germ theory. His work was funded by the German government. He developed a new way of studying bacteria which you might have used in your science lessons: **he grew them in dishes of agar jelly**. This provided food for the microbes as well as a stable surface which could be studied under a microscope. He also discovered that the microbes could be stained with dye so that they could be seen more easily. By doing this he discovered the microbes that caused anthrax in sheep, and later the microbes that caused tuberculosis and cholera.

Koch's work was picked up by other teams of scientists, who had isolated the microbes for half a dozen deadly diseases by the end of the nineteenth century.

Key term

Bacteria – another word for micro-organisms or germs.

Exam tip

Remember that identifying the microbe does not necessarily help to treat the disease! Tuberculosis is still an issue in some parts of the UK today, for example. Therefore it is important to bear in mind that, even though these discoveries were really important, their immediate impact on treatment was variable. However, they did have an impact on approaches to medical research.

Development of drugs and vaccines

Pasteur continued to experiment and, in 1879, he developed a vaccination for chicken cholera after it was discovered that exposing the microbe to air for a period of time made it weaker. Pasteur also used Koch's methods to develop a vaccine for anthrax using the microbes identified by Koch.

Koch worked with a team of research scientists, who continued his work and developed it further. For example, his protégé Paul Ehrlich discovered that certain dyes killed bacteria. This led to the development of the first magic bullet in 1911: Salvarsan 606 (see page 49).

Factors

- Pasteur was from France and Koch was from Germany. France had lost a **war** to Germany in 1871 and there was bitter rivalry between the two countries. This rivalry spurred both men to try to find cures for disease to glorify their countries.
- The rivalry also meant that both **governments** were willing to give Pasteur and Koch grants to fund research teams.
- Better **communications** also helped research teams worldwide to find out about and develop the ideas of Pasteur and Koch. Medical journals, such as the *Lancet*, and other scientific journals shared articles about the new discoveries which inspired other teams to carry out their own experiments.

> **War –** rivalry between France and Germany encouraged the scientists to work harder.

The importance of research teams in the development of germ theory and the discovery of the first microbes

Revised

- It was easier for research teams to get **funding** for expensive new technology like microscopes. This enabled Pasteur to observe the germs using the very latest technology: a microscope that magnified 1000 times.
- Research teams made it easier for scientists to **keep an eye** on each other's progress and methods to ensure everybody was working to the same high standard.
- Different team members could bring **different skills** to the research, for example biologists, chemists and doctors all had different knowledge and points of view.
- Younger scientists could work **very closely** with their bosses. This meant that when these more experienced scientists moved on or retired, their juniors were able to continue their work without interruption. For example, Paul Ehrlich was part of Koch's research team and went on to develop the first magic bullet.

> **Science and technology –** new technology made it easier to study microbes.

Revision tasks

1. Complete your medical megastar revision cards for Pasteur and Koch (see page 13).
2. Look carefully at the notes you have made. Who do you think had the bigger impact on medicine – Pasteur or Koch? Write a couple of sentences to explain why. This kind of thinking or argument will help you in your exam.

Exam practice

1. How much did the understanding of the causes of disease change between c1350 and c1900? *(12 marks)*

Answers online

Exam tip

To answer the exam practice question, you will need to look back through pages 25–33 to see what people believed caused disease from 1350 to 1750.

1. Begin by making a list of what people thought caused disease in 1350. (Tip: look at what people thought caused the Black Death.)
2. Then make a list of what people thought caused disease in 1900.
3. Compare your two lists to see if anything on them is the same.

Use this information to help you write your answer.

5.3 Improvements in hospitals and medical training

Church involvement in hospitals had declined after the Renaissance (see page 28). The gap was filled by charities, local people and town councils, which paid for hospitals to be set up. These were to provide both medical care for the sick and a place for doctors to train and carry out research. Doctors were now able to practise the medicine they had learned at university. Unfortunately, the growth in the British population in this time period, particularly in the cities, meant that there were not enough hospital beds to go round. Many sick people were still cared for at home. People who did not have anybody to care for them ended up in workhouses. However, some major changes took place in the nineteenth century which improved the situation for these people.

Key content

- How doctors built on Renaissance changes
- The impact of new technology
- Factors leading to improved medical treatment in hospitals

How doctors built on Renaissance changes

Revised

Renaissance scientists and doctors loved enquiry and experimentation. These things were equally popular during this time period.

- Anatomists like John Hunter – who was Jenner's teacher – carried out detailed **observations and dissections**, employing secretaries to write up their findings and artists to draw them.
- Doctors were required to **study medicine at university**; in 1815 the Society of Apothecaries and Royal College of Surgeons began to require students to pass examinations before being allowed to practise.
- Medical students still watched dissections as part of their training, but as time passed they were sometimes able to carry out their own dissections. When they were not provided with a body, they paid a **body snatcher** to acquire one for them.
- In 1858, the **General Medical Council** was set up to register all doctors.
- Following the development of germ theory, there was even more emphasis on observation. **Teaching hospitals**, where medical students shadowed doctors, began to grow in importance.

Over time, doctors became more professional, better able to treat disease and more widely respected in the community.

Exam practice

1. In what ways did the training of doctors change during the period c1350–c1900? **(12 marks)**

Answers online

Key term

Body snatcher – someone who stole the bodies of dead criminals or dug up recently buried corpses to sell the bodies, or pieces of them, to eager medical students.

Revision tasks

1. Write a list of how doctors were trained in 1350 (see pages 25–27).
2. Now write a list of training methods in 1750–1900 using the information on this page.
3. Highlight the similarities and differences in your two lists.

Exam tip

Try to group the information in your lists from the revision task – your **E**xamples – under one or two big headings, which will be your **P**oints. For example, one of these could be how much practical experience doctors had.

The impact of new technology

Revised ☐

- The **stethoscope** was invented in 1816; the modern version we would recognise today was developed in 1860.
- **Microscopes** became more powerful. In 1830, Joseph Lister developed one which magnified up to 1000 times.
- In 1866, Sir Thomas Clifford Allbutt invented a **clinical thermometer** which produced a patient's temperature reading within five minutes.
- In 1881, the first **device to measure blood pressure** was invented.

Science and technology – new inventions made it easier to diagnose patients.

Revision tasks

1. Look at the inventions above. Explain how they helped doctors with:
   a) observation
   b) enquiry.

2. Can you think of any other ways these inventions would have helped doctors to diagnose and treat their patients?

Factors leading to improved medical treatment in hospitals

Revised ☐

Attitudes and beliefs in society

Concern for the poor was fashionable in the nineteenth century. Social reform was spreading all over Britain and this had an impact on medicine. This was largely because the workhouses, meant to house the unemployed, were becoming full of the sick and disabled, who were unable to support themselves. Medical care was not very good in workhouses. The social reformers pressured local authorities and the government to improve matters.

Attitudes and beliefs – society began to worry more about the poor.

Government

The government acted on the pressure from social reformers and ordered the local Poor Law Unions to use funds from local rate-payers to build new hospitals and asylums for people who needed medical care. This was a major step for the government, who had previously had a laissez-faire attitude towards its people.

Government – attitudes changed. Governments wanted to help.

Role of individuals

Pasteur's germ theory led to hospitals being more aware of the link between dirt and disease and becoming cleaner places.

- New methods of sterilisation were introduced. For example, Joseph Lister used carbolic acid to create antiseptic conditions during surgery. Simple things like washing hands and boiling medical instruments became more common.
- Florence Nightingale's work in the training of nurses (see page 40) improved the standard of care in hospitals.

Role of individuals – doctors began to encourage hand washing.

Remember ...

It is important to remember that although people **recognised the need for better hospital care** by 1900, the standard was still not even close to what we have today. It took a lot longer for the government to act and create a proper system of hospitals and medical facilities.

Key term

Laissez-faire – meaning 'leave it alone', a key part of the government's policy in the nineteenth century. The government felt it was not its job to interfere in people's day-to-day lives by providing medical care.

Exam practice

2. Why did medical treatment in hospitals improve c1750–c1900?
   (12 marks)

Answers online

Exam tip

Use the factor headings for your **P**oints, the information in the boxes for your **E**xamples, and then **E**xplain by linking these back to the question.

5.4 Medical megastar: Florence Nightingale

Before the nineteenth century, women had been heavily involved in medical treatment within the home. However, they had been largely squeezed out of any professional kind of medical practice. Although women worked as nurses in private homes or in hospitals, nursing standards were not high and training was minimal. In the second half of the nineteenth century, Florence Nightingale was able to make significant changes to this situation.

Key content

- Florence Nightingale and nursing standards
- The role of women in medicine from 1350 to 1850
- The significance of the work of Nightingale

Florence Nightingale and nursing standards

Revised

Florence Nightingale felt called to the nursing profession, but her wealthy parents were very unhappy about this because at the time nursing was not considered a suitable job for an upper-class woman. Nightingale persisted though – she wanted to help people.

In 1854, Nightingale worked as a nurse on the battlefields of the Crimea but she was pretty disgusted with what she saw – typical conditions consisted of dirty wards and sheets, bad food and no privacy. Nightingale did not accept this. Her training in Germany had shown her the impact that bad conditions and poor nursing could have on the health of the patients. She used her own money to improve the conditions, for example she rebuilt a ward block and provided better meals for the sick. In spite of resistance from the doctors, the death rate fell sharply.

Nightingale felt that if she could have this impact in the hospitals of the battlefields, she could do it anywhere. When she returned to London, she gave a report to the government about what needed to be changed. For example, she recommended that hospital wards should have better ventilation and lots of light. Because she had already proven herself, it listened to her.

Revision task

Imagine you are reporting to the government on Florence Nightingale's behalf. Highlight three key pieces of information in the text that you would include in your letter. Then explain how each one shows that a change in nursing standards is important.

Role of individuals – Nightingale made nursing a serious profession.

The role of women in medicine from 1350 to 1850

Revised

The examiner might ask you how Florence Nightingale changed the role of women in the medical profession, so make sure you are clear on the role women had in medicine from 1350 to 1850.

- Women were **not allowed to attend university**, which meant that they could not train as doctors or practise medicine professionally.
- Most people who were ill stayed at home and were treated by the women of the family or **local healers**, who were usually women.

- **Wise women** provided herbal remedies and advice on curing illnesses and infections.
- Women acted as **midwives** and attended births until the seventeenth century, when it became fashionable to have a male doctor instead – for those who could afford it.
- **Nuns** nursed terminal patients in hospitals within their convents until the influence of the Church declined.
- **Wealthy ladies** provided medical care for the people on their family's lands and therefore often had some medical knowledge.

The significance of the work of Nightingale

Florence Nightingale played an important part in developing the role of women in the medical profession:

- Nightingale's methods eventually led to a 50 per cent drop in army hospital death rates.
- Her success was widely reported in the press, so people gave money to help her open the first school for nursing in Britain in 1861.
- Nursing became increasingly professional, and the role of nurses was valued more highly in hospitals.
- She wrote over 200 books on nursing and hospital design/organisation, which were popular all over the world.
- By 1901 there were 68,000 trained nurses in Britain – in 1850, there had not been any!

Revision tasks

1. Learn this acrostic to help you remember the significance of Florence Nightingale.

   Nightingale, first name Florence
   Unimpressed by the way nurses were trained
   Really wanted to do something about it
   So she sent a report to the government
   It got into the press, and people gave money for
   Nightingale's School of Nursing –
   Gave nursing a more professional feel

2. Create a timeline to show the actions that Florence Nightingale took to improve nursing. Add information to it from pages 40–41.

Exam practice

1. Describe the key features of the work of Florence Nightingale in the field of nursing. **(6 marks)**

2. How much did the role of women in medicine change between c1350 and c1900? **(12 marks)**

Answers online

5.5 Problems of public health c1750–c1900

By 1750 it was becoming more and more difficult for the government to ignore public health problems, and things only got worse. During the Industrial Revolution, millions of people moved to towns and cities. Living conditions were awful and public health became more of a problem. Although there were no more plague outbreaks, cholera regularly swept through the population. In spite of this, the authorities were slow to take action and it was only in the second half of the nineteenth century that significant improvements were made.

Key content

- Reasons why towns grew quickly 1750–1900
- Reasons why industrial cities were so unhealthy
- Reasons why governments were slow to clean up industrial cities

Reasons why towns grew quickly 1750–1900   Revised

In 1750 London was the only big city in Britain.

Most people in Britain lived in the countryside. Over the next 150 years that changed completely. By 1900 there were many cities. The population of Britain had expanded massively and most people lived in cities or towns.

This happened because of the **Industrial Revolution**. New factories needed lots of workers. People flocked from the countryside to the towns.

Industrialisation made Britain very **wealthy**, but to start with it made Britain's population very **unhealthy**.

> **Key term**
>
> **Industrial Revolution** – when British industry changed quickly and grew rapidly from 1750–1900.

Reasons why industrial cities were so unhealthy   Revised

Industrial cities had some similar problems to towns in the Middle Ages (only worse).

Then there were some new problems too:

- The factories were coal-fired and most people also burnt coal to heat their homes, so the air was filled with smoke and soot.
- Houses were put up quickly in the middle of towns, close to the new factories, so that people could walk to work. These were poor quality slums. There were no laws requiring the builders to provide clean water for the houses or sewage pipes to take the waste away.
- Overcrowded conditions helped disease spread quickly. Typhus, typhoid, diphtheria and tuberculosis were a constant danger. They were a particular threat to babies and young children.
- The change in the way people lived made a lot of people unhappy. Some drank gin, which was cheap and very alcoholic, to help them cope. Alcoholism caused further medical problems like miscarriage and liver problems.

Revision tasks

Picture what it would have been like to live in an industrial city in the early nineteenth century.

1. Draw a sketch to show the main risks to health. Include at least five risks that citizens would have come across every day.

2. Label them so you can remember them.

3. Underline those that were new in the Industrial Revolution.

Some attempts had been made to tackle health problems but they were not effective.

- Rakers now collected rubbish from people's homes. They left it near the edge of the city for passing carts to take into the countryside – but there was no organised system for this.

- People were supposed to pay night soil men to empty their privies, but many could not afford it.

- Private companies provided water to standpipes on street corners, but they were only turned on at certain times each day.

Key term

Privy – a toilet located in a small shed outside a house.

Reasons why governments were slow to clean up industrial cities

Revised ☐

Nowadays we expect government to be involved in every part of our lives. It is what governments do! So why did government not step in to sort these problems out?

- The government had a **laissez-faire** attitude. From the Middle Ages right into the nineteenth century the government left people or towns to solve their own problems. So there was **not enough desire** to tackle the issues. And local governments did **not have enough power** to enforce the rules.

- People could see from common sense that there was a link between rubbish and disease but they did not know what it was. They believed that miasma caused disease. So there was **not enough understanding**.

- Tackling public health is very expensive. Britain was getting richer through industry and trade but that money was in the hands of a few rich people who did not want to spend it on improving public health in the cities. They already felt they were paying too much in local taxes to support the poor. There was **not enough money** to do this.

Revision task

Here is a 'mud pie' to help you remember these points. In the industrial city there was plenty of mud but not enough

Money
Understanding
Desire
Power

Exam practice

1. Why did diseases such as cholera spread so rapidly in industrial towns during the nineteenth century? *(12 marks)*

2. 'The Industrial Revolution only made existing public health problems worse – it didn't create any new ones.' Do you agree? Explain your answer. *(16 marks)*

Answers online

5.6 Improvements in public health c1750–c1900

For centuries, British governments were unwilling or unable to improve public health. Then in the nineteenth century it all started happening because science gave improved understanding of disease; talented and committed individuals exposed the causes of the problems; and technology provided the tools to makes cities cleaner.

There were also some very specific events that triggered governments into taking action: for example, the **cholera** epidemic of 1837.

Key content
- How the government became more active in public health issues between 1750 and 1900
- How technology has improved public health
- Medical megastars: Edwin Chadwick and John Snow
- How crises triggered government action

How the government became more active in public health issues between 1750 and 1900

Revised

As small towns grew into massive unhealthy, industrial cities, the national government began gradually to take these problems seriously.

Key term

Cholera – a water-borne disease that brings on extreme sickness and diarrhoea. Sufferers die quickly from dehydration.

1831	**Cholera epidemic** – not the biggest killer disease but because it comes suddenly, and kills quickly, it is very scary. Also because it affects the upper classes as well as the poor, rich people take notice.
1837	**Cholera** returns and then again in **1838**.
1839	**Edwin Chadwick** (see page 46) is appointed by the government to lead an enquiry into the living conditions and health of the poor.
1842	**Chadwick's Report** on the Sanitary Conditions of the Labouring Population of Great Britain. This shocks the government into action. 20,000 copies are sold (not bad for a government report) and another 10,000 are given away. Chadwick believed in the miasma theory and so advocated cleaner streets and clean water supply as the way to improve health. He was wrong about the cause of disease but he was right about the actions. He also said something quite radical: that the poor were not to blame for their bad living conditions; that there was actually nothing the poor could do about it. It was the government that needed to act.
1848	**Cholera** returns and 60,000 die.
1848	**The first Public Health Act** is passed. This sets up a National Board of Health which has the power to set up Local Health Boards in areas with high death rates. These Boards can: • raise local taxes to make public health improvements • set standards for new housing such as having drains and toilets • appoint medical inspectors. Some towns such as Birmingham take action immediately and make big improvements. Others take no notice – it is too expensive.
1852	**Vaccination** (against smallpox) made compulsory. This is a sign of the government taking more responsibility for public health; however this law was not properly enforced until 1871.
1854	**Cholera** returns yet again, 20,000 die. During this epidemic **John Snow** (see page 46) proves that cholera is spread by infected water rather than by miasma.
1855	**Joseph Bazalgette**, an architect, is asked to draw up a plan for new sewers in London.

1858	**The Great Stink!** The summer of 1858 is really hot. The River Thames usually smells quite bad because all the city's sewage, industrial waste and rubbish is dumped there. In the extreme heat it smells worse than ever. Parliament meets right next to the river and MPs demand they move somewhere else. The Great Stink helps to stir the MPs into action and Bazalgette gets money to start building the new sewers.
1865	Publication of Pasteur's **germ theory**, which proves the link between germs and disease.
1866	Bazalgette's **sewers** completed. These pump sewage out of London towards the sea.
1866	**The Sanitary Act** requires all towns to appoint inspectors to keep an eye on water supplies and how waste is disposed of.
1867	Some working men living in towns are given **the right to vote**. From now on governments realise that to win elections they need to pass laws that help working people as well as the upper classes.
1875	**The Artisans Dwelling Act** gives local government the power to get rid of slum housing.
1875	**The second Public Health Act** forces local government to provide clean water, public toilets and proper drains and sewers, rather than just allowing them to.

We could sum it up like this: between 1750 and 1900 governments moved from **reacting to health threats as they arose** to trying to **prevent them before they happened.** And with this the old idea of laissez-faire died too.

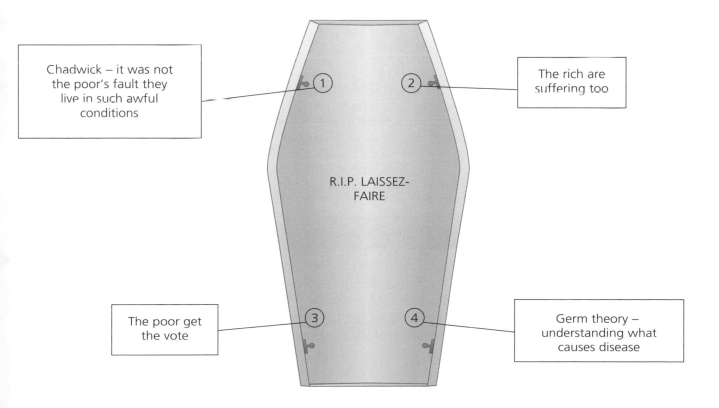

How technology has improved public health

Revised

Here are some good examples:

On page 31 you saw how the invention of **the pump** inspired William Harvey to look at the mechanism of the heart in a new way.

The pump had a more practical impact on health in the nineteenth century.

- In London powerful new pumps delivered clean water into cities at a rate of millions of gallons a day.
- They also removed the waste. Joseph Bazalgette's network of sewers, which opened in 1865, used pumps to send the sewage along the pipes far out of the city.
- A new **flushing toilet** was also invented, to take advantage of the new network.

Medical megastars: Edwin Chadwick and John Snow

Revised

In this period only one of the two candidates as medical megastars was a doctor. As the causes of poor health were better recognised, it became the job of the politicians and civil servants to push change through.

	Who was he?	What did he do?
Edwin Chadwick	A civil servant. He worked for the Poor Law Commission in the 1830s/40s. He became a member of the National Board of Health, set up in 1848. He wasn't very popular, though, and when this was disbanded in 1854 he retired from the civil service.	He wrote a 'Report on the Sanitary Conditions of the Labouring Population' in 1842. This said that the poor lived in terrible conditions which made them ill, and the rich should pay higher taxes to help the poor. He pushed the government to pass the 1848 Public Health Act after a cholera epidemic, although as we have seen, its impact was limited because it wasn't very strict.
John Snow	A doctor and surgeon. He theorised in 1849 that cholera was spread by water, not air – people just laughed at him.	In 1854, during a cholera epidemic, he mapped the deaths near his surgery and traced the outbreak back to one pump. He removed the handle and the outbreak died down. However, because this was before germ theory he couldn't prove why it worked – so it had little impact in the short term (other than preventing a lot more deaths, of course). However, he had proved that cholera came from water.

How crises triggered government action

Revised

Have you noticed how politicians are much more likely to take action about something if there is a sudden crisis rather than a long-term problem. Have you noticed too how politicians take action when their own or their political supporters' lives are affected personally by something? It was the same in the nineteenth century. Here are three important examples:

Cholera epidemics of 1831, 1837 and 1838

Cholera was such a sudden and shocking disease that it caused panic. It affected rich and poor alike. It affected politicians as well as voters. The arrival of cholera for the third time, in 1838, was what finally drove the government to order Chadwick's investigation.

The Great Stink of 1858

No one likes working in awful conditions, so when the Thames smelled so bad that Parliament could not meet, this helped trigger the building of sewers.

All working men get the vote in 1884

The 1884 Reform Act added millions of new voters. The government now had to take notice of problems that affected working people if they wanted to get elected. This helped lead directly to the second Public Health Act which made it compulsory for towns to make improvements to water supply, waste disposal and housing.

Revision task

On page 43 there was a mnemonic for the lack of government action before 1830:

M
U
D
P

Write a sentence or two for each point, explaining how this problem holding the government back was overcome in the nineteenth or twentieth centuries.

Exam practice

1. Describe the key features of John Snow's investigation into cholera in 1854. **(6 marks)**

2. How important was the work of Edwin Chadwick in improving public health in towns in the nineteenth century? **(16 marks)**

Answers online

Source A: Extract from *The Times*, 'Objecting to Sanitary Reform', 1854. A bumbaliff is an insulting name for a rent collector

'We prefer to take our chance with cholera and the rest than be bullied into health. There is nothing a man hates so much as being cleansed against his will, or having his floors swept, his walls whitewashed, his pet dung heaps cleared away, or his thatch forced to give way to slate, all at the command of a sort of sanitary bumbaliff. It is a positive fact that many have died of a good washing.'

Exam tip

This source gives you an idea of people's attitudes towards public health reforms in the nineteenth century, but it doesn't mention other issues. For example, this was published before germ theory. Make sure you place the information from the source into the **context** of the time period, using your own knowledge.

Exam practice

3. How useful is this extract (Source A) to a historian studying ongoing public health problems in the nineteenth century? Use Source A and your own knowledge to explain your answer. **(8 marks)**

Answers online

6 Medicine and treatment c1900 to present day

6.1 New drugs: from prevention to cure

The start of the twentieth century must have been a very exciting time to be in the medical profession. Jenner had shown that vaccination could work; now Pasteur had shown *how*. Thanks to Pasteur's germ theory, people finally understood what caused disease and this helped with research aimed at tackling it.

To start with, there was a lot of focus on prevention of disease by developing new vaccines. These were particularly aimed at diseases which affected children, such as diphtheria and whooping cough. The government's insistence on vaccinating the population against smallpox meant people began to see the value of vaccination, too.

Scientists also began to develop cures for people who had already been infected. This led to the discovery of the first antibiotics and the growth of the pharmaceutical industry.

Key content

- Further development of vaccines
- Magic bullets and their impact on medical treatments
- How penicillin was discovered and developed

Further development of vaccines

Revised

We have already seen how Pasteur and Koch competed with each other at the end of the nineteenth century **to see who could create the most vaccinations**. This **rivalry** led to huge leaps forward in medical knowledge with the development of new vaccines.

Many of the diseases that were the scourge of the population at the start of the twentieth century are now no longer a problem in the UK, thanks to the development of vaccines. For example, in 1913 Behring managed to produce a vaccine for diphtheria by isolating the anti-toxins produced by the body to fight disease.

As the century progressed, vaccinations were developed for other killers such as tetanus, whooping cough, polio and measles. This led to a decrease in rates of child mortality.

> **Exam tip**
>
> To remind you:
>
> A **vaccination** prevents you getting a disease. It does not cure you if you have already got it.
>
> A **magic bullet** is a chemical drug that cures you when you have already got a disease.

> **Revision task**
>
> In the section on Jenner there was a reminder to look at the long-term and short-term impact of his work (see page 35). The information above could fit into long-term impact! Go back and add to your medical megastar revision card for Jenner to help you remember the long-term impact of his work.

Exam practice

1. How important for the prevention of disease was Edward Jenner's discovery of a smallpox vaccination in 1796? **(12 marks)**

Answers online

Exam tip

When you are answering this question, you will need to look at both the short-term and long-term impact of Jenner's work. Now you have seen how other people built on his discovery, you should be in a better position to explain his importance in the long term.

Magic bullets and their impact on medical treatments

Revised ☐

After the discoveries of Pasteur and Koch, their research teams and other scientists, inspired by their work, focused on developing **cures** for major diseases. In addition to this, further research in chemistry and improved government funding led to discoveries which had a huge impact on medical treatment. These factors led to the development of the first chemical cures, or **magic bullets**.

Science and technology – new scientific discoveries improved medical understanding.

Government – more willing to fund medical research.

Key term

Magic bullets – chemical drugs which only killed the disease without affecting the person.

Exam practice

2. The table below shows two new medical treatments. Choose one and describe the key features of its development.
   - Salvarsan 606
   - Prontosil   **(6 marks)**

Answers online

Magic bullet 1: Salvarsan 606	Magic bullet 2: Prontosil
• Developed by Paul Ehrlich and his research team in 1909	• Developed by Gerhard Domagk in 1932
• Funded by the government	• Attacked the microbes which caused blood poisoning
• Combined dye with various chemicals to target only disease-causing microbes	• He was forced to test his compound on his own daughter who was dying from a pinprick on her finger – luckily it worked
• The 606th compound tested was discovered to be effective by Dr Hata, a member of the research team	• The active ingredient of Prontosil was isolated: sulphonamide
• This was very important: it was the first time chemical drugs had been used to cure illnesses	• Other sulphonamide drugs were developed to cure pneumonia, scarlet fever and meningitis

How penicillin was discovered and developed

Revised ☐

- An **antibiotic** is a drug used to treat infections caused by bacteria.
- Salvarsan 606 was the first successful chemical cure which targeted certain diseases. However, antibiotics are not created using chemicals but are produced by **micro-organisms**. Unlike Salvarsan 606, antibiotics can be used on a range of diseases. They use one sort of micro-organism to attack the harmful ones.
- The first antibiotic to be discovered and developed was **penicillin**, a naturally occurring mould. The timeline on page 50 shows how the properties of penicillin were discovered, and then developed into a cure.

For centuries, people had been making use of mouldy bread to treat infection. However, nobody knew how it worked.

↓

1928: A chemist named Alexander Fleming noticed that some mould in one of his petri dishes was killing his culture of bacteria. He thought this was quite interesting, and possibly significant, so he wrote up his findings and published them in 1929.

↓

1930s: Fleming could not get funding to develop his theory further. Everything went quiet for a bit.

↓

1939: Florey and Chain, two Oxford scientists, picked up Fleming's research. As the Second World War broke out, they received government funding to develop penicillin for use on humans. Florey and Chain and their research team grew penicillin in milk bottles and freeze-dried it. They tested it on mice. It was successful.

↓

1941: Florey and Chain had enough penicillin to test on a human. Their patient was seriously ill. The penicillin made him get a bit better – although unfortunately they did not have enough to cure him completely and he died.

↓

1942: The American government donated $80 million to drugs companies to fund the mass production of the drug. Penicillin was heavily used by Allied troops after D-Day.

↓

1945: After the war, the drug was mass produced for the civilian market.

Government – funded the research in 1939 (but only once the factor 'war' had intervened too! Sometimes factors work together).

War – high rates of casualties made better drugs a necessity.

Science and technology – new technology made it easier to produce and store penicillin.

Chance – Fleming's petri dishes were contaminated by chance.

Revision task

Remember that many factors led to the development of penicillin as a drug for the masses. Look at the boxes on the right to remind yourself what these factors were.

How many can you spot? Here is one to start you off:

War: The Second World War caused a lot of casualties. Many soldiers died of infections which could have been treated with penicillin. Therefore there was a very good reason to develop Fleming's research.

Add the rest of the information to your factors chart (see page 12).

Source A: Extract from a speech by Alexander Fleming, made in 1945

'The origin of penicillin was the contamination of a culture plate of staphylococci by a mould. It was noticed that for some distance around the mould colony the staphylococcal colonies had become translucent and evidently lysis was going on. This was an extraordinary appearance and seemed to demand investigation, so the mould was isolated in pure culture and some of its properties were determined.'

Exam practice

3. How useful is this speech to a historian studying the development of penicillin?

(8 marks)

Answers online

Exam tip

Remember to use your own knowledge to help you judge both what the source **does** tell you about the development of penicillin and what it **leaves out** – its limitations. For example, this source does not mention anything that happened after Fleming discovered the penicillin.

6.2 The discovery of DNA and its impact

There were massive strides forward in chemical cures in the first part of the twentieth century. Many diseases were being cured, which meant that scientists began to look more closely at what caused the diseases that **did not** respond to chemical treatment. Along with other important factors, such as the development of new **technologies** and increased funding from **governments**, this **scientific curiosity** led to the discovery, in 1953, of the structure of human DNA. DNA is what makes people who they are – and its discovery helped the medical profession to distinguish between diseases which were caused by external factors and diseases which were passed on genetically from generation to generation.

Key content
- The work of Watson and Crick
- The impact of the discovery of DNA on medicine

The work of Watson and Crick

Revised

Watson and Crick were scientists who worked together at the University of Cambridge. James Watson was a chemist and Francis Crick was a physicist. They are famous for identifying the structure of human DNA. Their research was helped by a variety of factors or people:

They built on a lot of discoveries around genetics that had been accumulating for a century. For example in the nineteenth century, a scientist named **Mendel** showed how characteristics were passed on from one generation to the next.

Improved **technology**, including X-rays and electron microscopes, allowed scientists to see human cells at a much higher magnification and take photographs to study. This was called crystallography.

It became widely accepted that each cell in the body contained DNA, which contained all of a person's genetic information. **Teams of researchers** worked to decode this information, hoping to be able to use it to tackle genetic conditions like cystic fibrosis.

A researcher at King's College, **Rosalind Franklin,** demonstrated her expertise with an X-ray and took some particularly detailed pictures of DNA. Watson and Crick studied Franklin's pictures carefully, and in 1953 were able to correctly identify the structure of DNA. It is a double helix, which can 'unzip' and make copies of itself.

Revision task

Try to decide which factor in the discovery of DNA was most important. Give each one a score out of 10 for how important it was. Would the work have taken place without the development of X-rays? How about if Watson and Crick had not worked with research teams?

Exam tip

Use the information from the revision task to help you write two strong paragraphs to answer this question. Remember not to spend too long on it, or provide a counter-argument: it is the least valuable question on the exam paper and you can score full marks just by showing off your knowledge.

Exam practice

1. Describe the key features of the work of Watson and Crick on DNA. **(6 marks)**

Answers online

The impact of the discovery of DNA on medicine

- **The Human Genome Project** – In 1986, the Human Genome Project began mapping the entire structure of human DNA. This took teams of scientists in eighteen countries fifteen years to complete. By the end of it, the purpose of every gene in the human body had been identified. This makes it easier to identify the genes that cause hereditary diseases.

- **Genetic screening** – It is now possible to test people who might carry a genetic disorder but are not affected by it, such as cystic fibrosis. It is also possible to test unborn babies for conditions such as Down's Syndrome. This raises a lot of ethical questions, but the science certainly allows people to be more prepared and informed.

- **Gene therapy** – This is the cutting edge of medical treatment. Research shows that normal genes from a donor could be taken and put into the DNA of someone who has a gene which causes a hereditary disease. This could prevent someone suffering from these illnesses. Another approach is the use of 'stem cells' which are taken from human embryos. These could be used to reverse a common form of blindness, or re-grow damaged cells to reverse paralysis. Again, there are lots of ethical questions surrounding this work.

Revision tasks

Create a memory map of the ways in which DNA has had an impact on medicine.

1. In the middle of a piece of paper, copy the memory map below.

2. Draw arrows pointing away from each impact and write notes about what they mean and how they changed medicine.

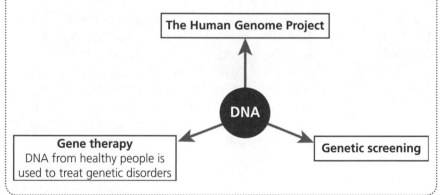

Exam practice

2. In what ways did the discovery of the structure of DNA change medicine after 1953? **(12 marks)**

Answers online

Exam tip

To answer this question, you need to write three good paragraphs using the **PEE** method. The **P**oints will be the three topics at the end of each arrow on your memory map. For each one, you will need to give an **E**xample of how it is used in medicine, and **E**xplain how this was a change in medicine.

6.3 The development of the NHS

Although there had been massive improvements in medical care during the nineteenth century, there was still a big gap between provision for the rich and for the poor. In the second half of the twentieth century, thanks in large part to the creation of the NHS, this gap has narrowed considerably.

Key content

- Why the National Health Service was established in 1948
- How the provision of medical treatments has changed for patients

Why the National Health Service was established in 1948

Revised

The 1911 National Insurance Act

The Liberal Government (1906–1911) made a lot of social reforms. One was the 1911 National Insurance Act. Employers, employees and the government paid into a **sickness fund**. This could then be accessed by people who needed to pay for medical care.

This was a step forward, but it only helped those in jobs. The unemployed were not part of it.

Government – began to provide more for its population.

The Second World War helps change attitudes towards healthcare

- During the war, many people were offered **free health care** to keep them healthy for the war effort. This increased people's sense of entitlement.
- Middle-class families were shocked at the condition of some of the evacuees from the cities who were dirty, unhealthy and undernourished. There was a growing feeling that good medical treatment should be **available to everyone**, not just the rich.

War – people became more positive about the idea of free health care.

The 1942 Beveridge Report

Sir William Beveridge (a civil servant) wrote a report on what could be done to improve people's lives. His report recommended:

- The creation of a **National Health Service**, paid for by National Insurance contributions and free to everyone. Doctors and nurses would be **employed by the government** instead of charging the sick a fee.
- Everyone in work would pay **National Insurance** out of their wages. This would help fund **benefits** such as sick-pay, pensions and unemployment benefit to everyone, whether they were working or not.

Role of individuals – Beveridge made the NHS look like it could work.

The work of Aneurin Bevan

The idea of the NHS was very popular, but there was some resistance.

- Doctors were unhappy about losing private, fee-paying patients.
- **Local authorities** were unhappy about losing control of their hospitals.
- Some thought the poor should **help themselves** instead of relying on the government.

Bevan was Minister for Health at the time. He made inspirational speeches in favour of the NHS, which won many people over. He also compromised with doctors by allowing them to continue treating patients privately and charging them fees.

Attitudes and beliefs – once doctors changed their attitudes, the NHS could work.

Exam practice

1. Why was it possible for the NHS to be launched in 1948? **(12 marks)**

Answers online

Exam tip

Your two **PEE**s for question 1 should focus on, firstly, what barriers to the NHS were removed by 1948 – you could talk about the change in attitudes after the Second World War – and, secondly, on the role of individuals like Bevan who made sure the NHS was launched in 1948.

Exam practice

2. Choose one of the following and describe the work he did which led to the creation of the NHS.

   - William Beveridge
   - Aneurin Bevan   **(6 marks)**

Answers online

Exam tip

For this question, you will need to explain both what your chosen individual did to enable the NHS to be launched, and then why it was important. For example, you might explain how Bevan helped to remove opposition from the medical profession.

How the provision of medical treatments has changed for patients

To begin with, all medical provision was covered by the NHS. However, costs began to soar and over time charges have been introduced for certain things, for example glasses, dentistry and prescriptions.

Today's patients benefit from an enormous range of treatments available on the NHS, from cutting-edge plastic and transplant surgery to alternative therapies, like acupuncture. Unfortunately, the NHS costs the government more every year, and funding it has become a major problem that needs solving.

Source A: A cartoon from *Punch*, showing Bevan feeding doctors from a bowl of soup labelled 'National Health Service', 1948

DOTHEBOYS HALL
"It still tastes awful."

Exam practice

3. How useful is Source A to a historian studying Bevan's role in the creation of the National Health Service?   **(8 marks)**

4. Why did the standard of medical treatment improve so rapidly during the twentieth century?   **(12 marks)**

Answers online

Exam tip

Question 4 also focuses on factors. Choose two factors that led to rapid improvement and give examples of the impact they had. For example, you might choose science and technology as a factor with the development of the magic bullets and the invention of new machinery as examples of how that factor led to rapid improvement.

6.4 The impact of new technologies

Every aspect of our lives has been affected by technology and medicine is no exception. In the first half of the twentieth century, there were breakthroughs such as blood transfusions and X-rays. In the second half, computers revolutionised diagnosis and treatment. High-tech medicine is effective but expensive and there are new ethical questions which we have to consider.

Key content

- The development of new technologies
- Problems created by medical advances

The development of new technologies

Revised

1900–1950

Blood transfusions

After the discovery of blood groups in 1901, **transfusion** was developed to treat patients with blood disorders, or who had lost a lot of blood. The technology for **storing blood** was developed during the First World War, when it was not practical to keep potential donors hanging around in the trenches.

Key term

Transfusion – a transfer of blood from one person or animal to another. Successful transfusions can only take place between two humans of the same blood type.

X-rays

We have already learned how X-rays contributed to the discovery of human DNA. They were discovered by a German scientist named Röntgen in 1895. X-rays were quickly put into use in hospitals to help **diagnose broken bones** and diseases. They were especially useful in the First World War, when the **government** funded X-ray machines for every major hospital on the Western Front. This contributed to their use in everyday medicine

Radiotherapy

Polish scientist Marie Curie developed **radiation therapy** from Röntgen's X-ray research. She and her husband discovered radium while using X-rays, which was developed to help diagnose and treat **cancer**. Often radiotherapy reduces the need for surgery. Along with **chemotherapy**, it has contributed to the survival of many cancer patients.

Science and technology – new machinery impacted diagnosis and treatment.

1950–2000

Medical scanning

Thanks to computing advances:

- X-ray technology is now employed in **CAT scanners**. These build up a 360° picture of a patient and help doctors to diagnose cancer and other illnesses in the early stages when they are still treatable.

- **MRI scans**, which employ magnets and radio waves, are particularly useful for examining the soft tissue.

Other medical technology

A variety of other new machines have been developed over the past century that are used in hospitals to help diagnose and treat various illnesses, for example:

- Endoscopes make use of fibre optics to help doctors examine a patient from the inside and perform keyhole surgery.
- Dialysis machines 'wash' the blood of people with kidney disorders.
- Pacemakers are fitted to treat patients with heart problems.

Home technology

Cheaper mass production techniques now mean that a wide variety of medical devices are available to use for home treatment. These include TENS machines to relieve pain, blood sugar monitors for diabetics, heart monitors and machines to monitor blood pressure.

Revision task

New technologies are helpful in both the diagnosis and treatment of diseases. Copy the table below and complete it with explanations of how each piece of equipment on page 55 fits into its chosen column. Challenge yourself to get as many pieces of equipment as possible into **both** columns. Finish by adding any other technological advances you can think of.

Diagnosing illness	Treating illness
X-rays are used in CAT scanners to diagnose cancer	

Exam tip

There are a lot of medical technologies to remember for this question. You should try to explain at least three in detail.

Here is a mnemonic to help you remember them.

Blood **T**ransfusions – **X-R**ay – **R**adiotherapy – **S**canning – **O**ther

By **T**he **C**ross **R**ed **R**uth **S**tepped **O**ver

Exam practice

1. In what ways has technology affected the treatment available to patients in hospitals since 1900? **(12 marks)**

Answers online

Source A: A seventeenth-century illustration of a blood transfusion from a lamb to a human

Source B: A patient receiving a blood transfusion in a modern hospital

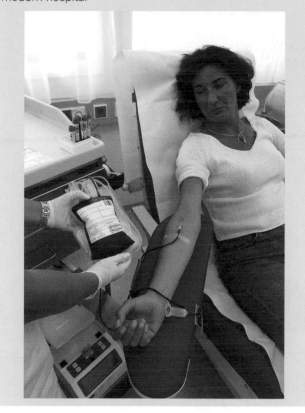

Exam practice

2. What do Sources A and B show about changes in the way doctors in Britain treat blood loss? Explain your answer, using Sources A and B and your own knowledge. **(8 marks)**

Answers online

Problems created by medical advances

Revised

- **Cost:** It can be very difficult to meet the cost of new equipment, particularly if it is very advanced and therefore expensive. Medical treatments such as IVF for infertile women are also very expensive.

- **Inequality:** High costs can lead to waiting lists and inequality of care. Wealthier people can seek private treatment, whereas those who cannot afford it have to wait for longer, or for a treatment such as IVF, have a limited amount of attempts.

- **Side effects:** New drugs often have unexpected side effects. We now have a rigorous testing regime for new drugs. However, in the past this has not been the case and has led to problems, such as the birth defects caused by thalidomide, an anti-sickness medication taken by pregnant women.

- **Ethical objections:** There is a lot of opposition to genetic research. Many see it as 'playing God'. Stem cell research can damage or kill the embryos providing the cells. Cloning, although already carried out in animals, raises huge ethical issues.

Exam tip

Your opinion on medical advances and the ethics surrounding them will vary hugely, depending on a wide variety of factors. As historians, it is important to try to consider several different points of view.

6.5 Public health c1900 to the present day

By 1900 clean water was available, sewers had been built and there were regular removals of rubbish. The government had dropped its laissez-faire attitude and started to make laws to ensure this stuff happened. Compulsory vaccinations had been introduced, so diseases like smallpox were a lot less common. Many previous problems had been solved.

However, there were other problems which still needed to be tackled.

> **Key content**
> - Government action to improve public health 1900–48
> - Government action to improve public health 1948 onwards

Government action to improve public health 1900–48

Revised

The Liberal reforms 1906–11

In 1906 a Liberal government brought in sweeping changes to try to **help the poor**.

1906	**Free school meals** were offered to children from poor backgrounds.
1907	The **School Medical Service** and **health visitors** were organised to check the health of young children.
1908	**Old Age Pensions** were offered to people over 70 who could not support themselves.
1909	**Back-to-back housing was banned**, and new regulations were brought in to make sure new houses were built to higher standards.
1911	**The National Insurance Act** set up a system of contributions from worker, employer and government, which then entitled the worker to free medical treatment and sick pay.

The interwar period 1918–1939

The government focused on building **a fit and healthy population.**

- School medical inspections were extended to children in secondary schools.
- Free milk was made available to primary-age children from 1934.
- Health clinics were set up to provide vaccinations.
- Local authorities began to take control of hospitals.
- Slums were cleared and nearly a million new homes were built.

Government action to improve public health 1948 onwards

Revised

The reasons why the NHS was created have already been covered in detail on page 53. It was all part of a massive set of changes that created the Welfare State to tackle the problems of disease, poverty, bad housing, unemployment and poor education.

The NHS revolutionised public health provision because for the first time everybody, rich and poor, had the same access to medical care.

Over the years, the NHS has focused also on:

- educating people about dangers to health so they can look after themselves, for example anti-smoking campaigns or promoting exercise
- vaccination programmes to tackle killer diseases
- screening programmes – to check for cancer or heart problems at the early stages.

The government also puts a lot of money into research to understand the causes of disease.

Through this period we could sum it up like this: in the twentieth century the government continued the nineteenth-century trend of preventing disease rather than reacting to it, but it looked even more deeply at the causes of ill health and tackled a much broader range of problems.

Science and technology – Computer **technology** has made it easier for people to access health care in their homes. NHS Choices, for example, enables people to look up their symptoms on the internet.

Exam practice

1. 'Public health problems had largely been solved by the twentieth century.' Do you agree? Explain your answer. *(16 marks)*

2. 'The government's role in improving public health was more important during the nineteenth century than the twentieth century.' Do you agree? Explain your answer. *(16 marks)*

Answers online

Exam tip

A 16-mark question will always ask you to build a balanced argument. Keep this in mind when revising: try to look at the positives and negatives of government intervention, for example.

Exam practice

3. How important was the work of Aneurin Bevan in launching the NHS in 1948? *(16 marks)*

Answers online

	Who was he?	What did he do?
Aneurin Bevan	Labour MP from Wales. Minister for Health when the NHS was introduced (1949). Inspiring speaker and idealist.	Bevan was very important in getting doctors on side when the NHS was launched. They were against the plans, partly because they were worried about losing money. Bevan compromised with them, and also encouraged patients to register for the NHS, which put pressure on doctors to join the NHS too. This contributed to it success.

Exam tip

Look back at page 53 to help you gather more information on the NHS for the last question. The table below is a reminder of the key facts about Bevan. Remember you need to build a balanced argument – so you could also talk about why the Beveridge Report was important.

7 The transformation of surgery c1845–c1918

7.1 Dealing with pain

The lack of effective **anaesthetics** before the nineteenth century held back the development of surgery. It was difficult to operate on a patient writhing in pain, so operations had to be quick, simple and not involve going too deep into the body. The most common type of operation at this time was amputation. However, thanks to some inquisitive surgeons carrying out experiments, this problem was solved by 1900.

Key content
- The first anaesthetics
- Medical megastar: James Simpson
- Why some people opposed using anaesthetics

Key term

Anaesthetics – drugs given to produce unconsciousness before and after surgery.

Exam tip

The historical Source Enquiry is all about how well you handle sources. As well as having some subject knowledge, you will also need to know how to look at sources and use them to answer exam questions.

The first anaesthetics

Revised

- **Nitrous oxide**, or laughing gas, was discovered to have anaesthetic properties by Sir Humphrey Davy in 1799. Some surgeons had some success with it, and it certainly reduced the pain suffered by patients, but it did not knock them out. This meant that its impact was limited.

- In 1846 an American surgeon named John Collins Warren used **ether** as an anaesthetic. It was a bit better than laughing gas as it made the patient unconscious. Famous British surgeon and showman Robert Liston used ether in an amputation in 1847. However, ether was an irritant that caused coughing and sickness. It was also very liable to catch fire.

Medical megastar: James Simpson

Revised

James Simpson discovered chloroform: the first effective anaesthetic.

This has to be one of the best medical stories of all time! A young Scottish surgeon, James Simpson, invited some other doctors round to spend an evening inhaling various chemicals to see what would happen. Can you imagine getting an invite to a party like that today? The police would break it up within minutes! But, this being the nineteenth century and as they were professionals, the party evening went ahead. At one point, Mrs Simpson thought it had all gone a bit quiet and walked in to find Simpson and his guests unconscious. They had inhaled chloroform.

Simpson realised that chloroform was a very effective anaesthetic and started using it during operations in 1847.

- It became popular after Queen Victoria used it during the birth of her eighth child in 1853.
- John Snow invented a special inhaler to regulate the dosage, which helped to prevent the heart problems some patients found affected them after using chloroform.

Revision task

Create a medical megastar revision card for James Simpson (see page 13).

Revision task

Draw a six-frame storyboard of the major events leading up to the discovery of chloroform. The first frame should show the problems surgeons faced due to the lack of anaesthetics. Remember to include laughing gas and ether in the story.

- Even though it was difficult to get the dose right and some people died during surgery after being given too much, this was still an enormous breakthrough. James Simpson was the first man to receive a knighthood for his contribution to medicine.

Why some people opposed using anaesthetics

Revised

- Some devout Christians thought that pain, particularly the pain of childbirth, was part of God's plan for human beings. We were supposed to feel pain! Some people even considered pain to be a blessing. However, Queen Victoria's approval meant the public were more willing to accept chloroform.

- You will know from the rest of your course that nearly all medical developments, however good they sound with hindsight, meet with opposition. This was also true of anaesthetics.

- In 1848, Hannah Greener died while being given chloroform during an operation to remove one of her toenails. The first death from using chloroform scared surgeons.

- The new anaesthetic encouraged surgeons to carry out more complex operations and go deeper into the body; but, since the problems of infection and blood loss had not been solved, this was not a good thing. In fact, in the 1870s the **death rate** from surgery reached a new high.

- Some doctors thought that an unconscious patient was more likely to die than one who was awake and screaming blue murder.

Source A: Letters published in the *Lancet* in 1849 and 1853. The *Lancet* was an important medical journal in which doctors shared details of their work

1. 'The infliction [of pain] has been invented by the Almighty God. Pain may even be considered a blessing of the Gospel, and being blessed admits to being made either well or ill.'

2. 'It is a most unnatural practice. The pain and sorrow of labour exert a most powerful and useful influence upon the religious and moral character of women and upon all their future relations in life.'

Exam practice

1. Look at Source A. What was the purpose of this representation? Use Source A and your own knowledge. **(8 marks)**

Answers online

Exam tip

Use both the information in the source and the provenance – what the source is and when it was written – to help you answer this question. Don't forget to bring in some of your own knowledge for context: you can only achieve a maximum of 6 marks if you don't do this.

Source B: Queen Victoria's remark, after being given chloroform during the birth of her eighth child

'Dr Snow gave that blessed chloroform and the effect was soothing, quieting and delightful beyond measure.'

Exam practice

2. Look at Source B. What was the purpose of this representation? Use Source B and your own knowledge. **(8 marks)**

Answers online

Exam tip

Unlike Source A, Source B shows a positive attitude towards chloroform. Think about the **impact** this praise from Queen Victoria would have had on people's attitudes and then you will start to understand the **purpose** of publishing it.

7.2 Dealing with infection

Following the development of anaesthetics, deaths from surgery increased. This was because surgeons did more and more complex operations but had not solved the problem of infection. In the 1890s surgeons still had very little understanding of how germs spread and what caused **gangrene** and **sepsis** – both big killers of surgical patients.

Even after the germ theory was published in 1861 (see page 36), it took six years for doctors to apply it to surgery and the treatment of patients. It was Joseph Lister who made the breakthrough and developed the first effective **antiseptics** and helped solve the problem of infection.

Key content

- Breakthroughs in dealing with infection before 1861
- Medical megastar: Joseph Lister
- How Lister changed surgery

Breakthroughs in dealing with infection before 1861

Revised

The way surgeons used to operate was pretty disgusting.

- They might have washed their hands in water (remember this water might itself be carrying infection).
- The instruments, table and operating room would not have been cleaned.
- Surgeons usually wore their oldest coat as a status symbol. This would have been covered in old blood to show how experienced they were.

Some people had made the link between cleanliness and better survival rates in hospitals.

Florence Nightingale (see page 40) ensured there were high standards of hygiene among her nurses and insisted that each hospital bed held only one patient.

In 1846, **Ignaz Semmelweiss** had noticed a funny statistic in his Austrian hospital. Women who were attended by midwives when they gave birth were much less likely to die from infection than those attended by medical students. This did not make sense, so he followed the medical students around for a few days. He realised that medical students often attended births straight from dissecting dead people. So Semmelweiss put bowls of chlorinated water all around the hospital and insisted medical students wash their hands. The infection rate fell dramatically.

People thought he was weird, though, because he could not explain why it helped. Also, the chlorine was really smelly. Semmelweiss was eventually sacked. However, some surgeons copied his ideas – James Simpson, for example (see page 60).

Medical megastar: Joseph Lister

Revised

Joseph Lister discovered that carbolic acid reduced infection. He championed antiseptic conditions in surgery.

Lister was a surgeon, and he read a lot of medical books. He had always wondered what caused infection, and read about Pasteur's **germ theory** soon after it was published in 1861. He thought about it a lot, trying to work out how it could lower the number of infections suffered by his patients.

Funnily enough, he got his idea from a very unlikely source – the **sewers. Carbolic acid** was used to kill parasites at sewage works, so he decided to try it out on the microbes causing infection. He tested it first on a child with a broken leg; the carbolic-soaked bandage meant that the wound, though very bad, healed cleanly within six weeks.

Excited about his success, Lister started washing his equipment and hands in carbolic acid, and treating the air around the patient during an operation with a **carbolic spray**. The death rate following operations fell dramatically. In 1867 he was able to proudly announce that no one on his wards had died from blood poisoning for nine months.

Lister went on to introduce **catgut**, which could be sterilised, to stitch wounds instead of silk, which could not be sterilised. Then he developed a type of catgut which dissolved in the body after a few days and did not have to be removed.

It was this sort of **practical application of new ideas** that led to Joseph Lister becoming Baron Lister in 1897. There is a special medal today reserved for the very best surgeons called the Lister medal. He even has an antiseptic mouthwash named after him. Can you guess which one?

↑ **Lister and the carbolic spray**

Revision task

Create a medical megastar revision card for Joseph Lister (see page 13).

How Lister changed surgery

Revised

To begin with, other surgeons were quite critical of Lister's developments (you are probably noticing a pattern of resistance to change). They did not like the smelly, corrosive carbolic acid and they did not believe it would help.

However, Lister's methods changed surgery. By the 1890s **antiseptic surgery** was common. This eventually developed into **aseptic surgery**, where germs were removed from the operating theatre, rather than the wound. Over the coming decades, hospitals became spotlessly clean; instruments were sterilised in boiling water or steam; sterile clothing, face masks and rubber gloves were introduced.

Key terms

Antiseptic surgery – killing germs on the wound.

Aseptic surgery – removing germs from the operating theatre.

Exam tip

This question is asking you to use a combination of your own knowledge and the source detail to answer it. Read the source and note down one or two points to explain why surgeons did not want to use carbolic acid. Then match these with one or two points from your own knowledge, using the information on these pages to help.

Remember to use own knowledge **and** source details – you cannot score more than 5 marks if you leave one of these out of your answer.

Source A: Taken from *Joseph Lister 1827–1912: A Bibliographical Biography*, by J.G. Bonnin and W.R. LeFanu, 1967

'The surgeon who operated in filthy clothes and a dirty room without the benefit of anaesthesia saw his results destroyed by infection and developed a hardness and lack of sensitivity ... When Lister showed that the surgeon should be and was responsible for the effects of the operation the wrath [anger] of many surgeons knew no bounds; they could no longer escape their responsibilities.'

Exam practice

1. Why were surgeons resistant to Lister's new methods? Explain your answer, using Source A and your own knowledge. **(10 marks)**

Answers online

7.3 Dealing with blood loss

By the end of the nineteenth century, blood loss was the only major barrier left to successful surgery. Surgeons had to be careful that the patient did not lose too much blood during an operation, as they were unable to replace it. Blood transfusions had been successful in the past, but they also failed sometimes for no apparent reason, which meant they could not be relied upon. Then, in 1900, Karl Landsteiner discovered blood groups, which made person-to-person blood transfusions possible. Once the technology was created to store blood, the issue of blood loss had been solved.

Key content

- Preventing blood loss before 1900
- Early experiments in blood transfusion
- Blood groups and the development of blood transfusions
- Blood banks

Preventing blood loss before 1900

Revised

To begin with, early surgeons prevented blood loss by using a method which is still used today sometimes – **cauterisation**. In this process, blood vessels are sealed shut by burning. Renaissance doctors used to do this with hot irons bars or by pouring boiling oil over a wound, which was horribly painful and did nothing to help the patient heal.

A sixteenth-century French surgeon, Ambrose Paré (pronounced Pa-ray), started treating his patients by clipping off blood vessels with metal clips, or by tying them shut with silk threads called **ligatures**. This was not terribly successful because it introduced more infection into a wound, but it was a step in the right direction. Lister later developed Paré's silk ligatures by using catgut, which could be sterilised more effectively (see page 63).

However, there was still no way of replacing blood that had been lost. Surgeons were reduced to applying a **tourniquet** or a clamp to reduce the blood flow to the area being operated on. They had to work quickly to avoid the patient losing too much blood.

Key terms

Cauterisation – using a hot iron to burn body tissue. This seals the blood vessels and stops bleeding.

Ligatures – a thread used to tie a blood vessel during an operation.

Tourniquet – a bandage used to apply pressure and restrict blood flow to an open wound.

Early experiments in blood transfusion

Revised

After Harvey had proved that blood circulated around the body (see page 31), other physicians started to attempt transfusions.

The earliest were **between sheep and humans** and were in some cases successful – but only because a tiny amount of blood was transfused. Other animal-to-person transfusions caused death and the practice was made illegal in Britain in 1670.

An American doctor, Philip Syng Physick, performed a successful **human-to-human** blood transfusion in 1795 and a British doctor, James Blundell, gave blood transfusions to ten people between 1825 and 1830. However, half of these transfusions led to death. We know today that this was due to a mismatch of blood groups, but nobody knew about blood groups until 1900.

Blood groups and the development of blood transfusions

Revised ☐

- In 1900, an Austrian doctor named **Karl Landsteiner** showed that there were different blood types, and that they were incompatible with each other. This was because the different antibodies in the blood groups reacted with each other. This was why some transfusions failed.

- Landsteiner's work made transfusions possible. In 1907 a New York doctor, **Reuben Ottenberg**, performed the first successful transfusion using blood typing. There was a problem, though: blood clotted when stored outside the body, which meant that the patient and the person giving the blood had to be together for the transfusion to take place.

Blood banks

Revised ☐

Person-to-person transfusions were fine, but they were not really possible in wartime on the battlefield. When the First World War broke out and hundreds of thousands of soldiers were dying from their wounds on the battlefields of Europe, scientists stepped up their search for a way to store blood for use later.

- In 1914, a Belgian doctor found that **sodium citrate** stopped blood from **clotting**. Others experimented with sodium citrate until the process was perfected and blood could be stored for several days after being removed from the donor.

- Then a process was developed for **separating the blood cells** from the actual blood. These could then be stored, packed in ice and diluted with saline to create usable blood. This made transfusions possible for thousands of wounded soldiers on the front lines.

- The British set up blood banks for use during the war. The first blood depot, set up in 1917, carried only blood type O, which can safely be given to other patients regardless of their blood type.

> **War** – During the First World War, the successful storage and transportation of blood became an urgent concern. This meant better funding for research. Without the war, the methods might have taken longer to develop.

Source A: Blood transfusion kits being packed at the British Army Blood Supply Depot

Source B: Taken from 'A Method of Citrated Blood Transfusion', by O.H. Robertson, published in the *British Medical Journal* in 1918. Robertson was the first doctor to use sodium-citrate-treated blood on soldiers during the First World War

'This method [of blood transfusion] was used under rush conditions. Forty-four transfusions were given to 38 patients. The patients transfused were cases of haemorrhage and shock – chiefly the former … the immediate effect of the citrated blood was the same as that seen after the transfusion of blood by other methods in common use.'

Exam practice

1. How reliable are Sources A and B as evidence of the changes in blood transfusions by 1918? Explain your answer, using Sources A and B and your own knowledge. **(10 marks)**

Answers online

Exam tip

When you're answering this question, use your own knowledge to judge whether the source details are accurate or not. This will help you to judge its reliability: if it doesn't match what you know, it's probably not reliable. Use the source provenance to help you too.

7.4 Factors influencing developments in surgery

You have probably got quite a full list of factors which have held back or pushed forward developments in medicine over the centuries. Which of these factors most helped surgeons solve the problems of pain, infection and blood loss between 1845 and 1918: **developments in science and technology**, **improved communications** or the horrors of **war**?

> ## Key content
> - The impact of the First World War on the development of surgery
> - The impact of communications on the development of surgery
> - The impact of science and technology on the development of surgery

The impact of the First World War on the development of surgery

Revised

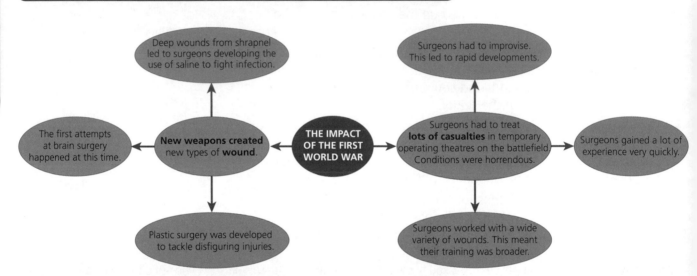

The impact of communications on the development of surgery

Revised

- Many surgeons took **careful notes** and encouraged people to take and publish photographs. Lister recorded the impact of his use of carbolic acid over several years, which helped him to prove that it worked.
- More scientists were **publishing their ideas**, sharing good practice and new ideas with doctors and surgeons. Medical journals such as the *Lancet* started to appear in the nineteenth century where surgeons could write about their

methods and success rate. This encouraged discussion of ideas among doctors.
- Medical **conferences** started to take place. Surgeons attended lectures given by other surgeons. Lister presented his work to Pasteur and 2500 other scientists in Paris in 1892.
- **Newspapers** reported notable operations, such as when Queen Victoria used chloroform during childbirth, and when King Edward VII had his appendix removed.

The impact of science and technology on the development of surgery

Revised ☐

- Developments in anaesthetics, antiseptics and the storage of blood for transfusions were greatly assisted by the study of **chemistry**.
- The development of **bacteriology**, a new science, helped doctors to understand what caused disease and infection. This in turn helped them to fight it.
- **X-rays**, developed after 1895, made it possible for surgeons to have a look inside the patient before they operated.
- The mechanism for **spraying** carbolic acid and the **steam steriliser** both helped to keep germs out of surgery, lowering infection rates.
- **Hypodermic needles**, invented in 1853, were useful in administering a measured dose of a drug. They were later used in blood transfusions.

Revision task

Make notes to explain how each of the factors of **war**, **communication** and **science and technology** affected:

- Pain
- Infection
- Bleeding

Exam practice

1. Source C suggests that better communication, using journals such as the *Lancet*, was the main reason for the development of surgery. How far do you agree with this interpretation? Explain your answer, using your own knowledge and Sources A, B and C.

   (16 + 3 marks for SPaG)

Answers online

Exam tip

These three sources all suggest very different factors that affected the development of surgery. You have three points of view to write about.

1. Begin by writing about improved communications and how this helped to improve surgery. Use Source C as a starting point and bring in some of your own knowledge to support it.

2. Now write about the impact of, first, war, using Source A and your own knowledge to explain the changes that had to happen because of the First World War. (Tip: you could write about blood transfusions here.) Then write about new technology, using Source B and your own knowledge.

3. Finish with a conclusion about which of these factors had the biggest impact.

Don't forget to bring in your own knowledge to provide context in this question. You can only score 10 marks if you don't do this.

There are 3 marks available here for your spelling, punctuation and grammar, so take particular care with your writing.

Source A: A patient being treated with pedicle tubes. This method of plastic surgery was developed by the surgeon Harold Gillies, who began to specialise in treating facial injuries during the First World War

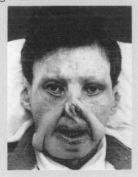

Source B: Spraying carbolic acid through the air. This new spraying mechanism was developed to allow Lister to create an antiseptic area around an operation

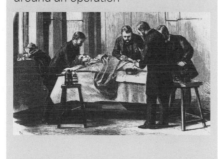

Source C: Extract from an online BBC article about the history of the *Lancet*, a medical journal which was launched in 1823, October 2003

'The Lancet, published in London, remains one of the most prestigious – and still attracts some of the most important announcements in medical science. When scientists traced the origins of the recent Sars outbreak, they communicated it urgently through the pages of the Lancet ... He [Thomas Wakley, the founder of the magazine] said that the weaknesses of "ignorant practitioners" could be exposed if doctors took more trouble to learn more about their subject ... In 1867, Dr Joseph Lister used the Lancet to publicise his new "antiseptic" to treat abscesses – another huge lifesaver.'

8.1 The Plains Indians: their beliefs and way of life

The **Plains Indians** were made up of around a dozen **nations**, all living in different areas on the Great Plains. Their civilisation had developed over centuries and had been shaped by the land they were living on. They had very different beliefs to the white settlers, many of whom thought of the Indians as savages.

Key content

- How the Indians lived on the Plains
- How the Plains Indians used the buffalo
- The beliefs of the Plains Indians and how they differed from those of the white settlers
- How Plains Indian society was structured

How the Indians lived on the Plains

Revised

- The simplest way to explain how the Indians were able to live on the Plains is **adaptation**. They **adapted** to their surroundings, using the resources available to them to help them survive.

- The biggest natural resource available to them was the herds of **buffalo**. The Plains Indians became very good at hunting the buffalo and made use of every single piece of the animal – they even burned the dung instead of burning wood.

- The buffalo provided the Plains Indians with their **tipi** homes, their clothes, their food and many everyday objects that made it possible for them to survive on the Great Plains.

- **Horses** made it easier for the Plains Indians to hunt the buffalo, and so they were considered an Indian's most valuable possession. Horses were so important that they were the equivalent of money to the Plains Indians – owning many horses showed that you were very rich.

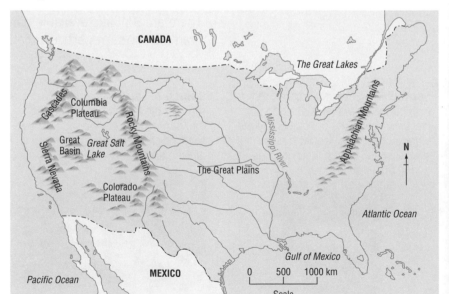

How the Plains Indians used the buffalo

Buffalo part	How it was used
Horns	For cups
Skull	Used in religious ceremonies
Rawhide (skin before being prepared)	For bags, belts, containers, horse harnesses, ropes, masks for ceremonial dances, sheaths, shields, snow-shoes, string
Tanned hide Leather	For bags, bedding, blankets, clothes, dolls, dresses, drums, leggings, mittens, moccasins, pouches, robes, saddles and, most importantly, tipi covers
Flesh	Some eaten fresh, the rest cooked, dried and mixed with fat and wild cherries to preserve it as pemmican
Dung	Used as fuel (buffalo chips) and smoked by men in special ceremonies
Bladder	For food bags
Fat	Used in cooking; to make soap
Bones	For arrowheads, knives, tools
Heart	Cut from the body and left on the ground to give new life to the herd. To the Plains Indians buffalo were sacred – man's relatives who gave their lives so people could live. The heart was also eaten raw so that the warrior could take the strength of the buffalo
Tongue	Used as a hairbrush or eaten raw as a delicacy

Revision task

Draw a diagram to help you remember how the different parts of the buffalo were used by the Plains Indians.

1. Draw a large buffalo in the middle of a piece of paper.

2. Label each part of the buffalo shown in the table left – insides **and** outsides.

3. By each label, write how the Plains Indians used that buffalo part.

Revision task

1. Make a large copy of the Venn diagram below which shows how the Plains Indians used the buffalo: for eating, living – anything the Indians needed day to day, like clothing and their homes – and religious/ceremonial occasions.

2. Fill in the spaces in the circles with key body parts and small drawings to show how the Indians used the buffalo. An example has been done for you to start you off.

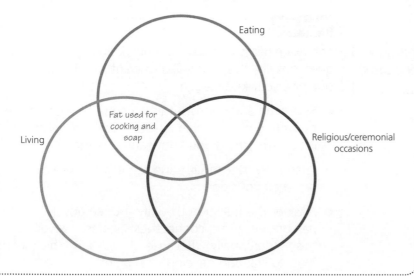

Exam practice

1. Why were the buffalo so important to the Plains Indians? *(12 marks)*

Answers online

Exam tip

When answering a question like this, break your answer into big categories first and then add your knowledge as support. For example, the big categories would be the headings you used in your Venn diagram: 'Eating', 'Living' and 'Religious/ceremonial occasions', and the supporting knowledge would be the labels you added.

The beliefs of the Plains Indians and how they differed from those of the white settlers

Revised

The beliefs of the Plains Indians and the things that were important to them were very different from the things that the white settlers valued. This led to conflict between the two sides. Three of the biggest differences were over **religion**, **attitude towards the land**, and **warfare**.

Religion

Plains Indians believed that everything in the world had a spirit, and that these spirits could influence events in the world. For example, before each buffalo hunt, the Plains Indians would hold a special ceremony called a Buffalo Dance to ask the spirit world for help. The spirits could also be contacted through visions. The tribal healers, or medicine men, were able to use power from the spirit world to heal illness.

The land

Because the Plains Indians believed that they were part of the land, they did not believe anybody could own it – that would be a bit like owning another person. High land, such as the Black Hills, was particularly sacred because it was closer to the spirit world.

Warfare

Since Plains Indians did not believe anybody could own the land, they did not fight over it. Instead, the Indians fought over horses or access to hunting grounds, to destroy their enemies and for revenge.

Being publicly shamed was one of the worst things that could happen to a Plains Indian, and this was reflected in the way they fought their wars. The bravest act in warfare, for example, involved getting close to your enemy and touching him with your hand or a stick. This was known as **counting coup**.

Revision task

One of the reasons for conflict between Plains Indians and white settlers was the differences in their beliefs. Complete this table to show how you think the Indians' beliefs differed from those of the settlers.

Beliefs about	Plains Indians	White settlers
Religion		
The land		
Warfare		

Exam practice

2. Describe the Plains Indians' beliefs about warfare. *(9 marks)*

Answers online

Exam tip

The examiner is testing your knowledge with 'describe' questions like this, but will also want to see that you can organise your knowledge.

- Save time and improve the structure of your answer by writing a short plan. This should be a bullet point list of everything you know about warfare.

- Then look over the list and see if you can make links between your points.

- Answer the question by writing three good paragraphs, using connectives such as 'As well as this', 'Additionally', 'Because of this' and 'This meant that' to link and develop your points.

Revised

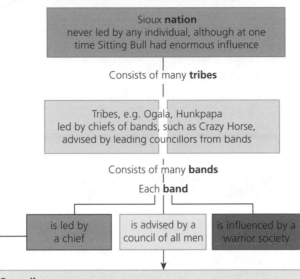

Sioux nation
never led by any individual, although at one time Sitting Bull had enormous influence

Consists of many **tribes**

Tribes, e.g. Ogala, Hunkpapa
led by chiefs of bands, such as Crazy Horse,
advised by leading councillors from bands

Consists of many **bands**

Each **band**

is led by a chief | is advised by a council of all men | is influenced by a warrior society

Chiefs
- Indian chiefs were not elected. They became chiefs because of their wisdom, their spiritual power of 'medicine', or their skills as hunters and warriors.
- They might not remain a chief for life.
- Only great chiefs like Red Cloud and Sitting Bull were able to persuade the warriors of many bands and even of different nations to follow them.

Councils
- Important decisions were taken in council, by the men of the band.
- The advice of the medicine men, chiefs and elders (old men) would be listened to with respect, but these men would not tell the others what to do.
- Normally, the council members would smoke a ceremonial pipe. The Indians believed that the smoke would inform the spirit world and help them to make good decisions.
- Sometimes councils were made up of all the men of the band; at other times only the important men would meet.
- Sometimes bands met together as **the council of the nation.** It could take important decisions, such as deciding to go to war, but the bands were not bound to agree with the council's decision. As a result, some bands might be at war whilst others were at peace. Later this was a source of confusion for the settlers when conflict broke out. Was a band at war or not? Were all its members peaceful or just some of them?

Warrior society
- Responsibile for supervising the buffalo hunt and preparing the band for travel. It also protected the band from attack.
- All the men in the band were members of the warrior society.

Punishment
If individual Indians did wrong and broke the 'rules' – by stealing, for example – they would be shamed or humiliated in the eyes of the rest of the band. These were the people with whom they lived and hunted all year round; many of them were their relations. So to be shamed would be a very effective punishment. In extreme cases, such as murder, some bands banished the wrongdoer. This was because a murder damaged the whole band.

Women
Although women did not have a place on the band's council, they were considered very important as they produced children. They owned and maintained the tipi, and fed and clothed the men and children in the band. There were more women than men as men were killed while hunting, so **polygamy** was allowed to ensure all women had husbands.

Exam tip

When you are thinking about how the social structure of the tribes made life easier for the Indians on the Plains, the key is to look at how it ensured every member of the tribe was taken care of. Remember that the most important part of Sioux life was following the buffalo, and think about how the structure of Indian society reflected that.

Key term

Polygamy – the practice of allowing men to marry more than one woman. It was also practised by the Mormons (see page 77).

Exam practice

3. Choose **one** of the following and explain how it helped the Plains Indians to live successfully on the Great Plains.
   - The social structure of tribes
   - Attitudes to land and nature   *(9 marks)*

Answers online

8.2 Migrants and settlers in the west: early settlers

In 1820, Major Stephen Long, a visitor to the Plains, described them as 'uninhabitable'. They were a windy, barren expanse of land, full of wild animals and savage Indians. Yet, by the end of the century, the Plains had been completely settled. This settlement began with people crossing the Plains to reach the rich farmlands and goldmines of Oregon and California, and the valuable animals in the Rocky Mountains. They laid down trails which were followed by millions later in the century.

Key content

- The first white settlers to cross the Plains
- Why the early settlers crossed the Plains
- The problems that were created by the California Gold Rush

The first white settlers to cross the Plains

Revised

The 49ers

After gold was discovered in California in 1848, **prospectors**, or gold seekers, flooded across the Plains to make their fortune. Around 90,000 people arrived in the state in 1849. Many failed to find the fortune in gold the guidebooks had promised. Guidebooks became popular in the mid-nineteenth century. Like very early versions of the *Lonely Planet* guides, these provided detailed advice about the journey and what settlers might expect in the West. They were written by people who worked as leaders for wagon trains.

Other settlers

Early visitors to the land on the Pacific coast, including explorers, fur trappers and mountain men, painted a very rosy picture of it. They reported that California was a land of sunshine and fruit trees, while Oregon land was perfect for farming. This sounded like a very tempting prospect to a lot of people living in the eastern states.

Why the early settlers crossed the Plains

Revised

The journey west was long, expensive and dangerous. The people who went needed some pretty convincing reasons to get up out of their armchairs and spend months in a bumpy wagon! Some of them were forced to go west by things that were bad about their circumstances in the east – we call these 'push' factors – while others were tempted to go west by things that were good about life in the West – we call these 'pull' factors.

Push factors	Pull factors
Economic depression In 1837, banks collapsed and there was massive unemployment. In Midwestern states along the Mississippi, the price of grain fell so low the farmers could not afford to sell it. These people had nothing to lose by moving west. **Overcrowding** Lots of people were moving to states on the edge of the Plains like Missouri, where the population increased by 2500 per cent between 1830 and 1840. Some of the residents started to feel a bit cramped.	**Propaganda** Good reports came back from people who had already moved to the Plains, making them sound inviting. **Government incentives** The Pre-emption Bill, passed in 1842, allowed people who squatted on land in Oregon to buy it very cheaply. For people who had lost all their savings when the banks collapsed, this sounded like a very good deal.

Exam tip

It is important to remember that these early push and pull factors **convinced people to cross the Plains, NOT settle on them.** On pages 81–82 you will review the factors that encouraged people to move onto the Plains themselves.

Revision task

Draw two stick figures, one to represent a gold miner and one to represent a farmer from the East. Give each one a speech bubble to explain why they chose to cross the Plains.

Exam practice

1. Why did early settlers move to Oregon in the 1840s? **(12 marks)**

Answers online

Exam tip

Divide your knowledge into sections to answer this question by using the **P**oint, **E**xample, **E**xplain method.

Point   Settlers moved to Oregon because they were pushed away from the east.

Example   For example, there was a terrible economic depression: banks collapsed and ...

Explain   This meant that people started to look west for new opportunities.

The Example section is where you demonstrate all your knowledge. Include as much as you can, but make sure you leave plenty of time to Explain at the end: this links the knowledge back to the question.

The problems that were created by the California Gold Rush

Revised

In 1848, gold was discovered in California. Within months, 40,000 men had crossed the Plains to get from the east coast to California with the sole aim of staking a claim to land in which they would find gold and make their fortunes (the **California Gold Rush**). This led to a massive increase in California's population, particularly in towns like San Francisco, which grew from a village of 200 to a city of 36,000 between 1846 and 1852.

Mining towns and villages were mostly made up of poor, single men desperate to get rich:

- They were living in **very basic housing** in racial groups who mistrusted each other.
- They were away from the **rules and regulations** of the East.
- There were **no effective laws or police** because the town had grown up so quickly.

- sometimes they got a **lot of money** all of a sudden and spent it very quickly.

This led to real problems of law and order:

- **Racial violence:** there were **many racial groups** – Europeans, people from the eastern states, Chinese, Mexicans, Indians. This was at a time when racial prejudice was common. This led to **violence between the groups** – bullying, chasing away from claims, banning from towns, murders.

- **Claim jumping:** people would often start digging on other people's land, or claim it was theirs.

- **Fights:** there was not much to do, but activities such as drinking, gambling and visiting prostitutes often led to fights.

Revision task

Create your own concept map showing the problems of law and order that were created by the Gold Rush. Use the headings in the diagram below to start you off.

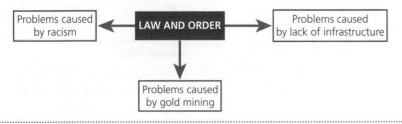

Exam tip

Both these questions test your knowledge recall. Question 2 can be answered using the information from the concept map. Remember the exam tip from page 70, and make sure you break your answer down into big sections, using the headings in the concept map to help you.

When you move on to question 3, highlight or underline all the information on these pages that might help you to answer it. Then, before you start writing your answer, go through the information and see if you can make any links between the points.

Exam practice

2. Describe the problems of law and order in California mining towns from 1849. **(9 marks)**

3. Describe the effects of the discovery of gold in California in 1849 on the growth of the American West. **(9 marks)**

Answers online

8.3 Migrants and settlers in the West: the journey west

North America is roughly 3000 miles across. Today, it would take you about four days on a bus to get from one side to the other, travelling on modern roads and with plenty of places to stop and refuel. The first travellers across the Plains did not have these luxuries, and the journey took six or seven months. Even good planning and preparation sometimes were not enough.

How the settlers made the journey west

Revised

The settlers usually travelled west in wagons, carrying with them everything they needed for the journey and their first winter in their new home. The wagons were usually pulled by oxen, which were strong and could be bred for meat at the end of the journey.

Settlers travelled in **wagon trains**. In April, these would leave from one of the frontier towns which could be reached by boat, such as Independence in Missouri. They would follow the route of the Platte River, resting at the US military forts along the way. It was really important that they reached and crossed the Rocky Mountains before summer finished, or they risked being snowed in.

Once past the Rockies, the wagon trains either headed northwest across the Blue Mountains and into Oregon, or southwest across a desert and the Sierra Nevada mountains, and into California.

Key term

Wagon trains – groups of wagons would travel in long lines or 'trains'. People could use the same guide and share resources, making the journey cheaper and giving them a better chance of surviving the crossing.

Exam tip

You can learn more about the dangerous journey west by going online and looking at this annotated Google map: http://g.co/maps/43ehz.

Source A: Excerpt from *The Prairie Traveller*, written by Randolph B. Marcy in 1859

'The day's drive should commence as soon as it is light and, where the road is good, the animals kept upon a slow trot for about three hours, then immediately turned out upon the best grass that can be found for two hours, thus giving time for grazing and breakfast. After which another drive of about three hours may be made, making the noon halt about three hours, when the animals are again harnessed, and the journey continued until night.'

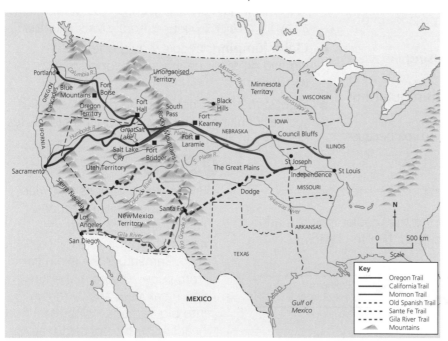

↑ The routes west

Exam tip

Don't think too deeply about this question: worth 4 marks, it should not take you longer than about five minutes to answer. A good way in might be to talk about how long they spent on the road each day.

Exam practice

1. What can you learn from Source A about the journey across the Plains? **(4 marks)**

Answers online

The problems that the settlers faced on the journey

- **Lack of supplies** – There were no shops or service stations along the way like there are today, so the wagon trains had few chances to restock. If they were lucky they would be able to buy supplies from the army at one of the forts, but these would be expensive.

- **Weather** – During the first part of the journey, which was across the Plains, the winds would often be high and there were some killer storms which could destroy wagons and cause cattle to stampede. During summer, the temperatures would soar and make the water shortages of the Plains much worse. Finally, if the wagon trains did not reach the mountains early enough, they might end up being snowed in.

- **Disease/accidents** – Lack of water made it difficult to keep clean, and with so many people travelling along the same routes there was a lot of poo about! This caused diseases such as cholera, which would kill within a couple of days and spread very easily. If a traveller was unlucky enough to be involved in an accident, lack of medical care often meant they died from wounds and broken bones which would have been treatable back in the east.

- **Attacks from Indians/wild animals** – Crossing Indian land could be dangerous: the Indians were suspicious of the wagon trains. The Indians were afraid the white settlers would take their land, or spread diseases. Sometimes the Indians wanted to trade with the travellers, but sometimes they did not. Wagon trains also had to be careful not to get caught up in the buffalo herds, which could easily destroy everything they owned.

- **Getting lost** – Although there were some maps, most wagon trains were led by guides who had travelled the route before. Sometimes, though, these guides tried shortcuts they had heard about, which led to disaster.

Revision tasks

1. Create a mind map of the problems faced by people on the wagon trains. Write 'Dangers of the Journey' in the centre and add lines to each of these key dangers:

Weather	**A**nimal attacks
Accidents	**I**ndian attacks
Getting lost	**D**iseases
Supplies	

   Add some key words and phrases for each danger.

2. Which problem do you think was the worst, and why? Pick one from your mind map and highlight the evidence which explains why. Practise your exam technique by making sure there are three key pieces of evidence to support your answer.

The Donner party

This is a good example to use to show the problems of travelling west. This group of pioneers were aiming to travel to California in 1846. They followed a shortcut which their guide, Hastings, had heard of. Unfortunately it proved to be much longer, and took the Donner party across the Great Salt Lake Desert, where large numbers of their animals died of thirst. This meant that they had to restock their provisions, which made them late reaching the Sierras. The snow arrived earlier than expected, and, trapped in the freezing cold with nothing to eat, they turned to cannibalism to survive. Only half of the 88 travellers made it to California.

Source B: Extract from Jane Gould's diary. Jane travelled to California across the Plains with her family in 1862

August 10

'We came to the Snake River. We learned that a train of eleven wagons had been attacked by Indians. The wagons had been plundered and all that was in them, and the teams taken and the men killed.'

August 13

'We came to a wagon that had been stopped. We saw the bodies of three dead men. They had been dead two or three weeks. One had his head and face cut out, another his legs, a third his hands and arms. Oh! It is a horrid thing. I wish all of the Indians in Christendom were exterminated.'

Source C: *An Attack on an Emigrant Train*, painted by Charles Wimar, 1856

Exam practice

2. What can you learn from Source B about the dangers facing travellers as they crossed the Plains? **(4 marks)**

3. What can you learn from Source C about the problems faced by wagon trains? **(4 marks)**

4. Describe the difficulties faced by people migrating west in wagon trains in the 1840s. **(9 marks)**

5. 'Getting lost was the biggest problem faced by people migrating west.' Do you agree? Explain your answer. **(16 marks)**

Answers online

Exam tip

A text source: When you have a piece of text to analyse as a source, start by underlining the key words in it. If you had to summarise the problems presented in Source B in one word, what would it be? You should state this when you start writing your answer.

Exam tip

A visual source: When analysing a source like Source C, start by saying what you see. Firstly, label the key features of the picture. Now, use the **PEE** method to structure your answer:

Point: Source C tells me that a problem faced by wagon trains was …

Example: For example, in the source I can see …

Explain: This was a problem for the wagon trains because …

Exam tip

A subject knowledge question: It is easy to get mixed up between problems faced by people travelling west and the problems they faced when they got there. Make sure the subject knowledge you use to help you answer this question is focused particularly on the journey.

Exam tip

A 'Do you agree?' question: This type of question is the most important on the paper – it accounts for almost one-third of the marks available! To achieve the highest marks, you need to create a balanced answer. Imagine your response is like a pair of balance scales.

One side of your answer needs to be that getting lost was the biggest problem migrants faced. The other side can be anything you like from the list of other problems. Make sure you write an overall conclusion, summarising your answer to the question.

getting lost ???

8.4 Case study: the Mormons

The **Mormon** religion was founded by Joseph Smith in New York State in the 1820s. Smith was an inspiring speaker and it did not take him long to build up a large number of followers. Unfortunately they were not popular in the east.

After Smith was arrested and killed by a mob, their new leader, Brigham Young, decided to move the Mormon community west to Utah, where they could practise their beliefs without interference. Their journey west was carefully planned and they were able to build a successful city around the Great Salt Lake.

Key term

Mormon – a member of the Church of Jesus Christ of Latter-Day Saints formally organised in 1830 by Joseph Smith.

Key content

- Why the Mormons moved west
- How the Mormons' journey was different from that of other settlers in the West
- Why the Mormons were successful in Salt Lake City

Why the Mormons moved west

Revised

Joseph Smith founded the Mormon movement in Palmyra, New York. He claimed that the Angel Moroni appeared to him and told him to create his own religion, because there was a lot of fighting going on among different sections of the Church at the time.

Smith's ideas became popular quickly and he gained a lot of followers. He hoped to build a Mormon city where they could practise their religion without interference from **gentiles**, but they were very unpopular and had to move three times. Smith himself was imprisoned more than once.

Key term

Gentiles – the name used by Mormons to describe non-Mormons.

In 1844 Smith claimed he had received a revelation from God, instructing him that some Mormons should practise polygamy. This split the Mormon community and his critics demanded that he be arrested. Whilst in jail, he was shot by a mob of gentiles protesting against polygamy and Mormonism in general.

Push factors	Pull factors
Unpopularity Mormons were unpopular for three reasons: a. The Mormons were quite successful and owned banks, mills and shops, causing jealousy among the gentiles (non-Mormons). b. The community was growing fast, thanks to missionaries in Europe. The gentiles felt threatened. c. Joseph Smith announced that Mormons should practise polygamy. This caused infighting within the Mormon community. It was also illegal under US law. **Persecution** The fear and jealousy felt by non-Mormons led to attacks on Mormons and the murder of their leader Joseph Smith in 1845.	● Utah was part of Mexico and therefore **not governed by the USA**. The Mormons would be able to practise polygamy there. ● Brigham Young, the new leader of the Mormons, had read that the Great Salt Lake was very **isolated**, **but** that the land was **fertile**. This must have sounded like paradise to a group of people who lived with constant persecution. Joseph Smith moved his followers as far as the Mississippi, but did not want to move the Mormons into the 'Great American Desert'. After he was killed, the way was cleared for a move west.

The Mormons started off in Palmyra, New York. They moved to Kirtland, Ohio; Independence, Missouri; and Nauvoo, Illinois before finally moving west to the Great Salt Lake, Utah.

Find these places on a map of the USA and plot their movements on the blank map below.

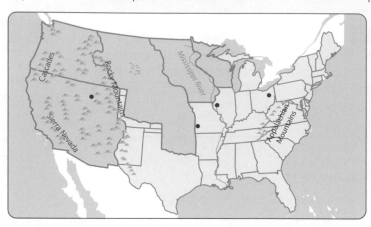

Source A: 'In Memoriam Brigham Young', by Joseph Keppler, 1877. Keppler founded a popular magazine in the USA which was designed to poke fun at politicians and other important people

1. What can you learn from Source A about the attitudes of gentiles towards the Mormons? **(4 marks)**

A lot of cartoons from the nineteenth century poke fun at the Mormons and their way of life – particularly their practice of polygamy. Remember that these cartoons are more useful for telling you about the **attitudes of gentiles** towards the Mormons at that time than about how the Mormons lived.

How the Mormons' journey was different from that of other settlers in the West

Brigham Young was very practical and well organised. He planned the move west very carefully.

Before the journey	• Wagons, oxen and supplies were all stockpiled in Nauvoo. • Pioneer bands were sent ahead to set up way stations along the route, so that the Mormons would be able to restock provisions along the way. • The wagons were divided into separate trains, each made up of 100 vehicles and led by a captain. Each wagon train had ten lieutenants who each supervised ten wagons.
On the journey	• The first wagon train built rest camps along the route for those following, leaving behind carpenters, blacksmiths and shelter. • Winter quarters were built next to the Missouri River to give the Mormons somewhere safe to spend the coldest months of their journey. • Young himself led a carefully selected band of pioneers ahead to the Great Salt Lake to start building the settlement.

It was not all good news. The freezing winter and the poor conditions of the winter quarters led to an outbreak of disease which killed 700 people. However, the Mormons were more successful in their journey west than many other groups of settlers.

Revision task

Look back at the details of a typical journey west (pages 74–76). Complete the chart below. Include each problem faced by the settlers in the West.

Problems faced by the settlers in the West	Did the Mormons solve this?	If yes, how?
Lack of supplies — running out of provisions		

Why the Mormons were successful in Salt Lake City

Stage One: Settling the Great Salt Lake

Brigham Young was a very level-headed man who planned carefully for the success of the Mormons at Salt Lake. For example:

- They banned private ownership of land or water, which meant that everybody worked together for the good of the population.
- Artisans and craftspeople had small plots of land towards the centre of the new city, while the bigger families had larger farms on the edges.
- Irrigation ditches were dug, which people could access only at certain times of the day to make sure everybody had enough water.

Stage Three: Settling the territory

Young arranged for new pioneer bands, containing a good mix of craftspeople and farmers, to found new towns all across the territory. He then set up the **Perpetual Emigrating Fund** and sent missionaries across the world to convert people to Mormonism and convince them to move to Utah.

Stage Two: Creating a new state

In 1848 the USA won the Great Salt Lake area from Mexico in a war. Young applied to form a new Mormon state called **Deseret**; although the US government rejected his proposal, they did allow the creation of the US Territory of Utah, with Young as the first governor. The Mormons now had the protection of the US government.

Key terms

Deseret – means 'honeybee'. If you go to Utah today, many of their road signs still carry a picture of a beehive.

Perpetual Emigrating Fund – lent money to settlers to pay for their journey to Utah. They repaid the money once they had settled in their new homes. This scheme was very successful: in 1855, over 4000 converts reached Utah.

Revision task

Brigham Young played an important role in the history of the Mormon movement and its journey west. In the exam you may be called upon to assess his impact. Here is a mnemonic to help you remember his key qualities:

DIPES:
Down-to-earth
Inspiring leader
Planned for the long term
Extremely well organised
Sensible

Now have a go at writing your own mnemonic to help you remember his actions.

Exam practice

2. Why was Brigham Young so important to the Mormons' successful settlement at Salt Lake City? **(12 marks)**

   You may use the following in your answer.

   - The Mormon Church shared out the land.
   - 1849: The Perpetual Emigrating Fund was set up.

   You must also include information of your own.

3. Why did the Mormons move to the Great Salt Lake in 1845? **(12 marks)**

4. Describe the key features of the Mormon journey to the Great Salt Lake. **(9 marks)**

Answers online

Exam tip

Look at question 2. The examiner will give you three bullet points to help you to answer this sort of question in the exam. These can be helpful if your mind has gone blank, but it is a better idea to see what information you can come up with yourself first.

8.5 Migrants and settlers in the West: settlers on the Plains

By the mid-nineteenth century, thousands of people had proved that crossing the Plains was possible. Oregon and California were full of settlements. The US government and population now turned their attention to what lay between the East and West: the Great Plains themselves. Over the next 40 years, thanks to some encouragement from the government and railroad companies and the pioneering spirit of the homesteaders, the Plains went from being a sparsely populated wilderness to the productive farmland that would help the USA become one of the richest countries in the world by the turn of the century.

How ideas about the Plains changed in the middle of the nineteenth century

Revised

By 1853, the USA controlled all the land from the east coast to the west coast, from its northern border with Canada to its southern border with Mexico. However, the government was nervous that it might not be able to keep control of all the empty land.

Enter **Manifest Destiny**! Although this phrase was originally coined by a newspaper editor, the government really liked the sound of it and used it to encourage people to move onto the Plains. By filling up all the space on the Plains with eager young homesteaders, the land would become more 'American' and less likely to be invaded successfully by another country.

To potential settlers, Manifest Destiny spoke to their patriotism. It was God's will that they should settle the whole continent, and they were doing their bit for freedom and their country.

Key term

Manifest Destiny – the belief that it was the right and duty of the USA to dominate the continent.

Exam practice

1. What can you learn from Source A about the idea of Manifest Destiny? **(4 marks)**

Answers online

Exam tip

This picture is very detailed and it would be easy to write a lot about what you can see. Instead, spend some time thinking carefully about what bits of the picture particularly fit with the idea of Manifest Destiny. Label these parts of the picture MD. Then use the **PEE** method to help you structure your answer.

Source A: *Across the Continent: Westward the Course of Empire Takes its Way,* painted by Frances Flora Bond Palmer, 1868

Why people moved to the Plains after 1860

Push factors	Pull factors
The Civil War When this ended in 1865, thousands of demobilised soldiers and freed slaves found they no longer had opportunities or a home in the East. Many of them set out onto the Plains to try to build a new life for themselves. **Problems in Europe** Rapidly increasing populations in European countries led to poverty and a 'land squeeze', particularly in England and Germany. There was a famine in Ireland. Jews emigrated to escape persecution.	**Success stories** Letters home from successful homesteaders, advertising by the railroad companies and the Plains states themselves, and enthusiastic articles in newspapers all made the Plains seem very tempting. **Government incentives** The government passed three laws to encourage people to settle on the Plains. ● **The Homestead Act**, 1862, allowed 160 acres of free land for settlers willing to farm it for five years. ● **The Timber Culture Act**, 1873, allowed settlers **another** 160 acres, as long as they planted 40 acres with trees. ● **The Desert Land Act**, 1875, gave settlers the right to buy 640 acres of land very cheaply in particularly dry areas, for example in the Southwest. **The transcontinental railroads** A railway across the continent was finally completed in 1869, making it easier for homesteaders to get to the Plains and also to return home to visit. The railroad companies spent a lot of money on posters to encourage people to use their trains. They also sold off the land next to the tracks very cheaply. Many European immigrants chose the USA because the railroad companies and **colonisation societies** advertised heavily in Europe and offered help and support to people who moved over.

Revision task

Create revision cards for the government Acts that gave away free land. On one side, write the name of the Act. On the other, write the details of the land available. You could draw a bird's eye view sketch of what the free land might have looked like, filling in trees or cactuses to help you remember. Here is an example to help you.

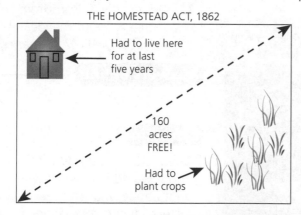

THE HOMESTEAD ACT, 1862

Had to live here for at last five years

160 acres FREE!

Had to plant crops

Key terms

The Civil War – 1861–65. In this war, 11 southern states (the Confederacy) fought the other 25 states (the Union) for independence. One of the main issues was slavery: the Union wanted to abolish it while the Confederacy wished to keep it.

Colonisation societies – charitable organisations which sponsored and assisted immigrants to the Plains. They were usually attached to a particular religion and aimed to bring more of their followers into their communities, making them stronger.

Exam practice

2. 'The government was the biggest factor in encouraging people to move to the Plains after 1860.' Do you agree? Explain your answer. **(16 marks)**

Answers online

Exam tip

Make sure you pay attention to any dates given in exam questions. There is a big difference between the factors that encouraged people to move to the west coast in the 1840s and 1850s and the factors that encouraged them to move onto the Plains themselves after 1860. For example, economic problems pushed the early settlers to the west coast, whereas after 1860 the Civil War was a more important push factor.

8.6 Farming on the Plains

Once they had made their journey and got their land **homesteaders** had a whole new list of problems to deal with. They had to build a house for themselves and their families, set up their farms from scratch and grow enough food to survive the following year. Many of the homesteaders were experienced farmers from the East, but this was not much help to them because farming on the Plains was very different. This was due partly to the extreme weather conditions and partly to the fact that the Plains had never been farmed before.

Key content

- The problems that homesteaders faced on the Plains and how they were solved
- The role that women played in Plains life

Key term

Homesteaders – settlers who acquired their own land which they farmed and built their homes on.

The problems that homesteaders faced on the Plains and how they were solved

Revised

Problems	Solutions
Lack of water The climate of the Plains meant low rainfall and dry summers. There were few rivers or lakes. This was a problem as water was necessary for growing crops, drinking and keeping clean.	**Dry farming** This method involved ploughing after rainfall, which trapped a layer of moisture underground where it could not evaporate in the sun. **The self-governing windmill** Developed in 1874, this pumped water up from underground for use on crops.
Lack of wood Wood was needed to build houses or fence land.	**Sod houses** These were built out of square blocks of earth cut from the ground, or 'sods', plastered together with wet mud and roofed with grass. **Barbed wire** Invented in 1874, this provided a strong alternative to wooden fencing and stopped livestock and buffalo from eating crops. **Buffalo chips** Dried buffalo dung made a good alternative to wood for fires.
Failing crops Traditional crops grown in the east were not hardy enough to survive extreme Plains weather.	**New crops** European settlers brought new crops with them from Ukraine, such as hard winter wheat which grew well on the Plains. **Livestock** Homesteaders began to keep cattle and sheep as well as growing crops, just in case the harvest was bad.
Tough land The Plains had never been farmed and the ground was too tough for traditional ploughs.	**The sodbuster** A new type of plough called 'the sodbuster' was invented by John Deere, which was strong enough to cut through the tough ground.
Bad weather Extreme heat in the summer was followed by extreme cold in the winter, and it was often very windy. **Natural disasters** One example was plagues of grasshoppers.	Unfortunately, neither of these problems had solutions and the homesteaders just had to put up with them. In years when the conditions were good, they worked hard to **grow a surplus** which they could sell to buy better machinery, or store in case the following harvest was a bad one.

The most successful homesteaders on the Plains were the ones who **adapted**. Like the Indians, they had to change the way they lived to suit their surroundings.

It was not an easy life and a lot of people gave up and went back east; but for those who were able to stick it out, the rewards were rich.

Create a concept map of the problems and solutions faced by the homesteaders on the Plains. In the middle of a piece of paper, write the word 'Problems'. Draw arrows around it and write a problem at the end of each one. Now expand your map out another layer by drawing arrows from each problem to its solution. Draw a little picture to go with each problem and solution to help you remember it.

Here's a fake web address to help you remember the problems: www.ctn.prob
Water, **W**eather, **W**ood; **C**rops, **T**ough land, **N**atural disasters.

Exam practice

1. Why was it so difficult for the homesteaders to settle on the Plains in the 1860s? **(12 marks)**

2. 'Technology was the most important factor in solving problems faced by homesteaders in the 1870s and 1880s.' Do you agree? Explain your answer. **(16 marks)**

Answers online

Exam tip

Using the right connectives can be the difference between 11 marks and 16 marks in question 2. If you are following the **PEE** method you will have well-structured explanations; now make sure you link them using some good connectives, for example:

- On the one hand
- Furthermore
- As well as this
- Also
- Equally
- On the other hand
- However
- Alternatively
- Another point of view is
- Therefore
- Overall
- In summary

The role that women played in Plains life

Revised ☐

The free land offered under the Homestead Act was available to women as well as men. For this reason, a lot of men married before moving west, so that the couple could claim 320 acres between them.

The day-to-day work of women on the Plains was quite similar to the work they would have been used to in the east: cooking, cleaning, having children, raising the family and keeping the sod house comfortable. However, this only represented a small part of what Plains women would be expected to do.

- **Keeping the kitchen and fire stocked** – Women often tended their own gardens of fruit and vegetables, as well as fishing and gathering wild plants from the surrounding prairies. They also collected buffalo chips to burn for fuel.

- **Making do and mending** – To begin with, supplies of everyday items such as soap, candles and clothes would have been very limited.

Women made their own where possible, and patched and darned garments until they fell apart.

- **Building communities** – The early mining communities were almost all single men, and this led to lawlessness. Once the women arrived, however, a better sense of community developed. On the Plains they had to work hard to develop these communities. Homesteaders had to live on their land according to the terms of the Homestead Act, which meant that life could be very lonely. Usually it was the women among the homesteaders who organised social gatherings, set up and ran schools, and built the communities which soon began to flourish on the Plains.

Occasionally, single women would move to the Plains and set up their own farms. In fact, some historians estimate that around 12 per cent of homesteaders in the northern Plains were single women.

Revision tasks

1. Draw a series of stick figures to represent women completing various tasks on the Plains. Give each one a speech bubble to explain what she is doing.

2. How important do you think women were in life on the Plains? Make a list of how life might have been different if only men had lived in the communities, like the early mining communities.

Exam practice

3. Describe the contribution made by women to settling on the Plains. **(9 marks)**

Answers online

Exam tip

Use your answers to the two revision tasks to help you organise your answer to this question. Women had two roles: helping to build communities and carrying out everyday tasks. Make sure you have a section of your answer dedicated to each.

9 Development of the Plains

9.1 The construction of the railroads

Between 1850 and 1890, nearly 140,000 miles of railway track was laid across the American continent. The railroads became a key factor in the settlement of the Plains. They helped people to move, supplied them with goods once they got there and shipped their produce off to the profitable markets in the eastern states. They also helped the US economy to grow and speeded up its industrial revolution, so that by 1890 the USA was the world's leading industrial power. It was thanks to the vision of a few railroad 'barons' and ongoing support from the government that they were built.

> **Key content**
> - Why people wanted the railroads to be constructed
> - The problems faced by the railroad builders
> - The impact of the railroads on the inhabitants of the Plains

Why people wanted the railroads to be constructed

Revised ☐

The US government

The government was very keen to see the railroads spread across the whole country.

- They would help to fulfil **Manifest Destiny** by making it easier for people to settle across the whole continent.
- They could improve life for the people already living on the Plains, by helping the government to bring **law and order** to the settlements.

The US government hoped the railroads would help strengthen the economy.

- They would create thousands of **jobs** and increase demand for raw materials such as steel and timber.
- They would help the USA to **trade** with countries on the other side of the Pacific such as China and Japan.

The railroad companies

The US government offered huge incentives to any company able to complete a transcontinental railroad. They gave away free land to build on, which could be sold for a profit: after all, only a small strip along one edge of the land was used for the tracks! The companies also stood to profit from the railroads once they were finished through ticket sales and commercial haulage. The first transcontinental **railroad companies** were the Union Pacific and the Central Pacific.

> **Key term**
>
> **Railroad companies** – the two railroad companies that were set up after Congress passed its Pacific Railways Act in 1862 were the **Union Pacific** and the **Central Pacific**.
>
> - **Central Pacific** worked from Sacramento in California towards the east.
> - **Union Pacific** worked from Omaha in Nebraska towards the West. Eventually the tracks met at Promontory Point, Utah.

> **Revision task**
>
> Create a diagram to show the reasons why the government wanted the railroad to be built, and the incentives they provided to the companies. Draw a set of six boxes and see how many different reasons you can provide from the information above. For example, the first frame could show a railroad stretching out across the new land, similar to the Manifest Destiny picture on page 81.

↑ **The route of the transcontinental railroad**

The problems faced by the railroad builders

Landscape
The railroad crossed deep valleys, treacherous mountains and dry deserts. It took a long time and a lot of skill to build tracks through these places.

What problems did the railroad builders face?

Worker shortages
With conditions so bad, it was no surprise there was a shortage of labour. The railroad companies brought in thousands of immigrants from China and Ireland to help lay the track.

Working conditions
Railroad workers lived in awful conditions. They usually inhabited shacks or tents by the tracks, which were no protection against the terrible Plains weather. They were also regularly harassed by Indians.

Money was not a problem. Investors were very keen to invest.

Source A: Plaque next to a section of the original Transcontinental Railroad in California

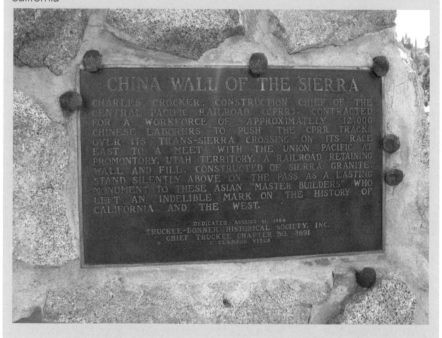

Exam practice

1. What can you learn from Source A about the building of the railroads?
   (4 marks)

Answers online

Exam tip

This source commemorates some of the workers who built the railroads. That is the key piece of information that will help you answer this question. You can extend your answer by making suggestions about why railroad companies employed these people rather than white Americans.

Exam tip

Prioritise the information you use to answer this question. Start with the most important factor and then work through the ones you think are less important. Then, in your conclusion, you can summarise by referring back to your first paragraph.

Exam practice

2. Why was it so difficult for the railroad builders to complete the transcontinental railroad? *(12 marks)*

Answers online

The impact of the railroads on the inhabitants of the Plains

Homesteaders

The railroads benefited those farming on the Plains in two ways.

- **They brought in lots of new goods.** Supplies of everyday items such as clothing and kitchenware, and farming items such as wind pumps and ploughs, flooded onto the Plains. This made day-to-day life easier and enabled farmers to grow more crops.

- **The railroads took crops away.** Homesteaders were now able to sell their surplus in the eastern states, where demand was higher. This meant they got a better price for their produce and were able to plough the money back into their homesteads, creating a bigger surplus the following year.

Cattle ranchers

- The railroads allowed cattle ranchers from Texas to move their animals to the more profitable markets in the east without having to drive them over 1000 miles to the nearest train stations in the Midwest.

- The invention of the refrigerated railcar in 1880 made the process even easier, as cattle could be slaughtered and butchered before being shipped. As a result, huge cow towns sprang up near the railroads.

Immigrants

- The US government granted the railroad companies land in a chequerboard along the route of the tracks.

- Each plot of land was 10 miles by 10 miles, and the railroad companies sold them at a bargain rate. Often they would organise whole colonies of immigrants from Europe into communities.

- Most homesteaders lived on their farms, miles from their nearest neighbours, so these new communities helped to increase the growth of towns and other settlements on the Plains.

Indians

- Just about the only group of people who did not benefit from the new railroads were the Indians. Since the railroads helped the new settlements to grow, the land available for the Indians to live on became smaller and smaller.

- There were also special train excursions for buffalo hunters, which led to a huge drop in the number of buffalo on the Plains.

Key terms

Cattle ranchers – people who own (or manage) large farms (ranches) where cattle are bred.

Cow towns – where cattle drivers could meet up with cattle buyers.

Revision task

Can you write a series of rhymes to explain how the railroads helped the Americans settle and live on the Plains? Refer to different groups of people in your answer, for example homesteaders, railroad builders and immigrants. Here is a 'ranchers' example of a limerick to start you off:

The ranchers made use of the trains
To move the cows east from the Plains.
The cows, they stayed healthier,
So the ranchers got wealthier,
They were definitely using their brains!

Exam tip

It is really important to remember that although the railroad was useful for transporting people and goods onto and across the Plains, the cheap land, the jobs and the demand for things like steel were just as important in helping the white settlers take control of the whole country.

Exam practice

3. Choose **one** of the following and explain how the building of the transcontinental railroad changed their lives.

   - The homesteaders
   - The Plains Indians

   (9 marks)

Answers online

9.2 The rise and fall of the cattle industry

In the first half of the nineteenth century, cattle ranching developed in Texas. Cattlemen bred cows to sell for food, and quickly realised that a cow would fetch a better price in the East than in Texas. Therefore, they started to experiment with different ways to get their cattle to the eastern states. They began by driving their cattle to the railroads, and as these spread across the Plains these cattle drives became shorter. In the 1870s, some cattle ranchers claimed land on the Plains and began to set up their ranches there. The industry was very profitable until a fall in demand, coupled with some very severe weather, led to the end of the cattle boom in the late 1880s.

Key content

- The reasons why there was a boom in cattle ranching after 1865
- The factors that led to the spread of cattle ranching to the Plains
- How the cattle industry changed the settlement pattern on the Plains
- Why the cattle industry eventually fell into decline

The reasons why there was a boom in cattle ranching after 1865

Revised

New breeds – A new breed of hardy cow was developed which was able to survive the tough conditions in Texas. It was called the Texas Longhorn. Longhorns thrived in the tough conditions of the state, which quickly became a major centre for cattle ranching.

The Civil War – Many Texan ranchers left their herds for four years during the Civil War. When they came back, the herds had done what comes naturally, and Texas was now teeming with cows – nearly 5 million of them. Something had to be done with them.

The growing demand for beef – Beef became a popular food in the East. The government bought a lot of cattle to feed the army, and the Indians on the reservations. The railroads bought cattle to feed their workers.

The factors that led to the spread of cattle ranching to the Plains

Revised

As with the homesteaders, some cattle ranchers were 'pushed' onto the Plains, while others felt themselves 'pulled' onto them.

Push factors (Reasons to leave Texas)	Pull factors (Reasons to ranch on the Plains)
Negative impact of cattle drives Cattle had to be driven over 1000 miles to Illinois to the nearest railroad station. This took a long time. Many cows died on the way and they all lost a lot of weight, which made them less valuable. Ranchers were forced to look for alternatives.	**Free land** There was a lot of open space on the Plains. Cattlemen could claim their 160 acres of free land, and claim on behalf of their cowboys and ranch hands as well, combining the land into huge super-ranches.
Conflict with homesteaders on the Long Drive As homesteaders spread across the Plains, they fenced off their land to prevent cattle drives from trampling their crops. They were very unfriendly to the cattlemen, because the cows carried a disease called Texas Fever, and they did not want this to spread to their own cattle. Therefore, the homesteaders would block access to water and grazing on the main cattle routes north.	**The weather** The lower Plains temperatures killed off the ticks that caused Texas Fever, leading to healthier cattle.
	The railroads Once the new railways crossed the Plains, cattlemen decided it would be even easier to raise the cattle by the railroads, instead of driving them up from Texas.

Key terms

Cattle drive – this did not involve a contest to see how many cows could be squeezed into a car! Cattle were herded north by cowboys to reach the rail routes to the markets in the East.

The Long Drive – movement of cattle from the open range in Texas to the markets (and, later, to railheads).

Revision task

Draw a staircase to represent the growing number of cattle on the Plains. On each step, write a reason why cattle ranching spread to the Plains. How many steps can you make?

Exam practice

1. Describe the factors that led to the spread of cattle ranching onto the Plains. **(9 marks)**

Answers online

Exam tip

Use your completed steps diagram from the revision task to help you answer question 1.

How the cattle industry changed the settlement pattern on the Plains

Revised

To begin with, the cattle industry led to the growth of new towns close to the railroads, called cow towns. The first of these was Abilene. They were full of stock pens and lodgings for cowboys, and were ideal as a place to which the ranchers could drive their cattle and wait for a train to take them East. These new towns became important hubs in Plains life.

After a while, cattlemen started to set up their own ranches on the Plains. These **open range** ranches often covered thousands of acres and were home to a new type of worker to the Plains: the cowboy.

Key term

Open range – the name given to the ranches of the nineteenth century because they had no specific boundaries. Instead, different herds of cattle would mingle with each other, and be rounded up once a year to be sold. Ranchers branded their cattle with a unique mark, so that they could tell which cows belonged to them. There are some places in the USA where open range ranching is still practised.

Why the cattle industry eventually fell into decline

Revised

CATTLE RUSTLING: Protecting cattle was almost impossible on the open range.

1880–85

- **OVERGRAZING:** Ranching made lots of money, so more people became ranchers. By 1882 there were too many cattle and **not enough grass** to feed them.
- **BAD WEATHER:** There was a **drought** in 1883 which meant that a lot of the grass withered.
- **FALLING BEEF PRICES:** Beef became less popular in the East. Supply outstripped demand. The price of beef began to fall and ranchers earned less for their cattle.

↓

1885–87

- **MORE BAD WEATHER:** Two very cold winters and a hot, dry summer killed grass and many cattle.

↓

The end of the open range

The cattlemen realised that they needed to **look after their cattle and the grass**, so they began to **fence off their own land**. This meant they could:

- breed their cattle selectively to produce better meat or more milk
- use wind pumps to get water from deep in the ground
- grow better grass to feed their cattle.

Exam practice

2. Why did open range ranching decline after 1883? **(12 marks)**

Answers online

Exam tip

The cattle industry did not decline for just one reason, but because of a combination of different factors. This is an ideal opportunity to show off your ability to link reasons together.

9.3 Cattlemen and cowboys

The biggest factor in the growth of the cattle industry was the number of people willing to work and invest in it. A few key individuals acted as trail-blazers. They made their new ventures into great successes, which meant that other people wanted to follow in their footsteps. Alongside them worked hundreds of cowboys. These were often ex-soldiers, criminals or immigrants who could not find regular work elsewhere. These men looked after the enormous herds. Without them the industry would have ground to a halt. Small wonder, then, that they became romantic heroes in novels about the Wild West.

Key content

- The impact of key individuals on the cattle industry
- How life for a cowboy changed

The impact of key individuals on the cattle industry

Revised

Charles Goodnight	Joseph McCoy	John Iliff
• Cattle rancher from Texas • Along with his partner, Oliver Loving, **he was the first to drive his cattle to Fort Sumner, New Mexico in 1866** • Once there, he sold his cattle to the US army to feed their soldiers and the Indians on the reservations • Others followed his example and by 1870 the US government was buying 50,000–60,000 head of cattle a year	• Cattle dealer from Chicago • **Founder of the first cow town**, Abilene, in 1867. He filled it with stock pens which encouraged ranchers to drive their cattle there • He provided a meeting place for the ranchers and buyers from the northern and eastern states • Between 1867 and 1881, nearly 1.5 million cattle passed through the town instead of being driven to more distant cattle stations	• **The first big rancher on the Plains** • He began ranching in 1862 • He built up his herd by buying lame and footsore animals from the cattle drives • Eventually he had a herd of 35,000 cattle and major contracts with the railroad builders and the Sioux Indians • He set a good example: other ranchers followed him to the Plains

Exam practice

1. Choose one of the following and explain his contribution to the growth of the cattle industry on the Plains.

   - Charles Goodnight
   - John Iliff **(9 marks)**

2. 'The work of Joseph McCoy was the most important reason for the development of the cattle industry.' Do you agree? Explain your answer. **(16 marks)**

Answers online

Exam tip

You can use your answer to question 1 to help you with question 2. Remember that this needs to be a balanced answer: one side of your argument will cover the work of Joseph McCoy, and the other can be about the work of the individual you picked for question 1. Don't forget to write a summarising conclusion at the end.

How life for a cowboy changed

Revised

The role of the cowboy changed over time, keeping pace with the changes in ranching through the second half of the nineteenth century.

Cattle drives

To begin with, the main job of the cowboys was to round up the cattle and drive them north to the railroads. They had to supervise the cattle on the routes north, protecting them from natural hazards such as bad weather, fast-flowing rivers and wolves. It was hard, dangerous work. Sometimes the herds would be attacked by Indians looking for food. Occasionally a herd would stampede and the cowboys would have to risk their lives to round them up again. Even at night they could not fully relax, because the cattle had to be guarded.

Cowboys were usually paid when they reached their destination, and would often spend all their wages in one go. This gave cow towns such as Abilene a bad reputation, because the drinking and gambling often led to violence.

Open range ranches

Once the ranches moved out onto the Plains, the role of the cowboy changed a little. They were responsible for making sure the cows on the ranch were kept safe and healthy. They still rounded up the cattle, branded them and drove them to the markets, but as these were now much closer this took less time. Cowboys who worked on these ranches would live in bunkhouses or in line shacks on the boundaries of the ranch.

Fenced ranches

Once fencing was introduced to cattle ranches, there was less demand for cowboys. Boundaries were now protected by barbed wire, so cattle could not stray and rival herds could not graze on the ranch. The cowboys who were left continued to ride around the ranches looking for sick or trapped animals, and they were now also responsible for mending the fences. However, the era of the cowboy was over.

Source A: *Laugh Kills Lonesome*, c1925

Source B: *Gunfight*, 1902

Exam practice

3. What can you learn from Source A about the life of a cowboy? **(4 marks)**

4. Why did the lives of cowboys change in the period 1875–95? **(12 marks)**

   You may use the following in your answer.

   ● 1874: Barbed wire starts to be made.
   ● 1886–87: The harsh winter killed many Longhorn cattle.
   You must also include information of your own.

Answers online

9.4 Law and order: problems and solutions

We have already seen on page 73 how law and order was a problem in the first mining settlements during the California Gold Rush. The situation was not much better in the cow towns that sprang up across the Plains. Because the cattle drives were seasonal, thousands of cowboys would turn up all at the same time, and they would all have money to spend on drink and women. This led to a lot of violence in towns which often had little or no law enforcement. For example, roughly 5000 cowboys turned up in Abilene in 1871. From 1872, the town banned cattle drives.

Key content

- The problem with law and order in Plains settlements
- The different types of law enforcement
- The role that vigilantes played in keeping law and order

The problem with law and order in Plains settlements

Revised

Distance

Towns were far apart and it took law enforcement officials a long time to get to places. If a new **federal** lawman turned up and the townspeople did not like him, it was easy for them to get rid of him and say he had never turned up. Accused criminals had to wait a long time for their cases to be heard as there were not enough judges and sometimes people took matters into their own hands.

Demographics

Lots of different people lived on the Plains, and they did not always get on.

- There was racism towards **immigrants**, particularly from China and Mexico, and towards ex-slaves.
- There was a high population of **young, single men**, who came to the Plains without wives and families and spent all their money drinking and gambling.
- There were also many **ex-soldiers** from both sides of the Civil War.
- This led to a lot of social tension in many areas of the Plains.

The law of the gun

There was a primitive code of honour in the west. It was your responsibility to settle things for yourself. If you shot a man carrying a gun, you could claim self-defence and get away with it. Life was cheap.

Key terms

Federal – the federal government is based in Washington DC and oversees law and order for the whole country. In addition to this, today states have their own government and sometimes there are also city governments.

Demographics – the different types of people that make up a population in an area.

Revision task

Imagine you are a concerned citizen living in a Plains settlement. You want to write a letter to the government to explain why you think there are problems with law and order in your town. Highlight three problems in the text (left) that you would talk about in your letter. Then think about what could be done to solve them.

Exam tip

You could use the three problems you wrote about in your letter from the revision task as the basis for three paragraphs to answer this question.

Exam practice

1. Describe the problems of law and order in the cow towns on the Plains in the 1860s and 1870s. **(9 marks)**

Answers online

The different types of law enforcement

Revised

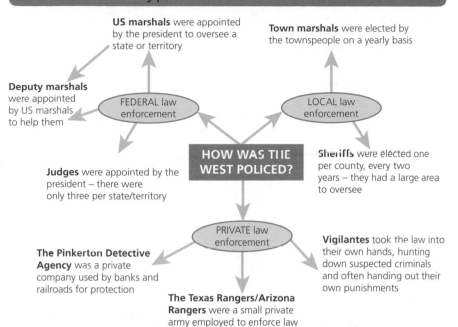

US marshals were appointed by the president to oversee a state or territory

Town marshals were elected by the townspeople on a yearly basis

Deputy marshals were appointed by US marshals to help them

FEDERAL law enforcement

LOCAL law enforcement

HOW WAS THE WEST POLICED?

Sheriffs were elected one per county, every two years – they had a large area to oversee

Judges were appointed by the president – there were only three per state/territory

PRIVATE law enforcement

Vigilantes took the law into their own hands, hunting down suspected criminals and often handing out their own punishments

The Pinkerton Detective Agency was a private company used by banks and railroads for protection

The Texas Rangers/Arizona Rangers were a small private army employed to enforce law

Revision task

Townspeople often considered their local law enforcement to be very corrupt. Local landowners were able to get away with murder, by bribing lawmen to turn a blind eye. Look at the diagram on the left of the different types of law enforcement: which officials do you think would have been easiest to bribe? Why?

The role that vigilantes played in keeping law and order

Revised

Vigilantes often acted as law enforcers when the official lawmen were not seen to be doing a good job. We still have people like this today, who talk about hunting down criminals and giving them a proper punishment. However, because we have a good police force and a clear system of law in Britain, they cannot get away with it.

This was not the case in the West. Sheriffs were often corrupt or open to bribes. Federal law enforcement was too scarce and did not command enough respect. Vigilante groups would spring up, often led by the richest and most respectable men of the community. This was because those men had the most to lose from **rustlers** and other criminals.

In some places vigilantes were welcome, and seen as a force for good. However, suspected criminals were often lynched without being given the chance to defend themselves in a fair trial.

Revision task

There are lots of interesting characters in Wild West history. People like Billy the Kid, Wild Bill Hickok, Pat Garrett, Jesse James and Wyatt Earp were the subjects of countless dime novels which painted a romantic and exciting picture of the Plains. Do some of your own research into a few of these characters so that you have examples of lawbreakers and lawmen to include in your exam answers.

Key terms

Vigilantes – people who were willing to take the law into their own hands. This might have happened because they were unhappy with the work of the local lawmen, or in areas where there was not enough law enforcement.

Rustlers – people who stole cattle from herds. In reality, an unbranded cow was not actually owned by anybody, but the ranchers did not see it like that, especially as many rustlers built up their own herds this way and were then competing for the same grazing land.

Exam tip

When writing your answer to question 2, look back at the information about the life of cowboys on pages 90–91. Remember that their brief visits to cow towns would be the busiest and most lawless time of year. Make sure you include this when you explain why law and order was a problem in cow towns.

Exam practice

2. Why was it so difficult to keep law and order in the cow towns? **(12 marks)**

3. Choose **one** of the following and explain their importance in dealing with lawlessness in the American West.
   - Vigilantes
   - Sheriffs and marshalls **(9 marks)**

Answers online

9.5 Law and order: conflicts

Until the cattle ranchers arrived on the Plains, most conflict was small-scale, between homesteader families or between homesteaders and Plains Indians. The nature of Plains settlement meant that people did not live close enough to each other for conflict to be a huge problem. However, as more people began to make demands on the land, conflict became more common. The cattle ranchers were unpopular with the homesteaders. They fought among themselves and with other types of farmer for access to drinking water and grazing.

Key content
- Why the cattle ranchers created conflict on the Plains
- The impact of the Johnson County War on the cattle industry

Why the cattle ranchers created conflict on the Plains

Revised

The cattle ranchers did not arrive that much later than the other settlers. However, they were in competition for the same land with homesteaders and other farmers, which led to conflict.

Conflict with homesteaders

To start with, ranchers got into trouble with homesteaders when they drove their cattle across the homesteads to get to the markets. The cattle **trampled crops** and **spread disease**. These conflicts were part of the reason the cattle drives ended.

Once the ranchers had moved to the Plains, they had very different ideas about what a good farm looked like and this caused further conflict. They did not want fences put up and they were very keen to make sure they had access to the precious **water supplies**. When homesteaders did fence their land, cattle ranchers often sneakily cut the **barbed wire**. This caused further tension and conflict.

At the end of the open range (see page 89), the ranchers started fencing off enormous pieces of land for their ranches. Now it was the homesteaders' turn to use the wire cutters!

Conflict with sheep farmers

Sheep farming became popular on the Plains in the 1880s and was more of a threat to the ranchers because sheep and cattle were competing for the same grass. There was quite a lot of violence from the ranchers towards the sheep owners: they would kill shepherds, burn fodder and slaughter sheep. The fact that a lot of shepherds were Indian, Mexican or European did not help matters.

Conflict with rustlers

The cattle ranchers were very worried that their young, unbranded cows were being stolen by rustlers and often acted brutally to ensure this did not happen. The Johnson County War is an example of one such conflict.

Revision task

Create a cartoon storyboard with pictures of all the causes of conflict between cattle ranchers, homesteaders and sheep farmers. Draw a series of six boxes to begin with, leaving yourself some space to add extra if you need to. In the first box, draw a stick man to represent a homesteader and another to represent a rancher; give each figure a speech bubble to explain why they are arguing.

Exam practice

1. Why was there so much conflict between the cattle ranchers and other settlers on the Plains? *(12 marks)*

Answers online

Exam tip

Look at your cartoons from the revision task and select the three factors you feel most confident about. Develop these into paragraphs to answer this question, using the **PEE** method.

The impact of the Johnson County War on the cattle industry

Revised

The Johnson County War took place in Wyoming in 1892. A number of cattle barons, tired of not having everything their own way, took matters into their own hands and aimed to rid the whole county of rustlers. This was vigilante justice at work.

Wyoming Stock Growers Association (WSGA)

Formed in the 1870s, this was a group of very powerful cattle barons who got together to protect their interests. Members included the governor and state senators. Between them, they claimed most of Johnson County as their land. By the 1880s they had three problems.

New settlers: Homesteaders and small ranchers were moving to Wyoming and settling on land the cattle barons claimed was theirs.

Rustling: A 'maverick' (motherless calf) could be claimed and branded by anyone. Many people started their herds this way. The cattle barons saw it as stealing, but it was very difficult to prosecute the offenders.

Falling prices: Cattle ranching was in decline, due to falling demand in the east. The cattle barons were losing money.

The Wyoming Stock Growers Association decided to take matters into their own hands. They hired a gunfighter to hunt down the rustlers.

In 1889, two people accused of rustling – Jim Averill and Ella Watson – were lynched outside their home. They were living on land claimed by cattle barons. Ella was a prostitute who apparently accepted cows for her services.

By 1892, the cattle barons began planning a full-scale invasion of Johnson County to drive the rustlers out. They planned to capture the town of Buffalo, kill the sheriff and round up the 'criminals'.

The WSGA drew up a death list and hired 25 gunfighters, offering bonuses for every rustler killed. They then cut the telegraph wires, cutting Johnson County off from the outside world, and set off for Buffalo.

The invaders arrived at KC ranch. They were delayed by Nate Champion and Nick Ray who fought to the death to stop them getting any further. Some passers-by realised what was happening and rode to Buffalo to raise the alarm.

The invaders approached Buffalo, but realised the townspeople were armed and ready. They retreated to the TA ranch, where they were besieged by nearly 300 men. The US cavalry had to come and rescue them.

As you can see, things did not go well for the Wyoming Stock Growers Association! However, they never faced trial so in a way they got away with it. The incident was a huge embarrassment to the governor and the other members who held political office, and they could no longer openly support the local cattle barons. Without any powerful friends, they had no influence, and small ranches and homesteads continued to enclose their land. This event marked the beginning of the end of the open range in Wyoming.

Revision task

Many historians consider the Johnson County War as a key event in the decline of cattle ranching on the Plains. Look back at the reasons for the decline of cattle ranching given on page 89. What do you think the most important reason was? Explain your answer.

Exam practice

2. Describe the part played by the cattle barons in the Johnson County War in 1892. **(9 marks)**

3. Describe the impact that the Johnson County War had on open range ranching **(9 marks)**

Answers online

Exam tip

The key thing with the Johnson County War is the impact it had after it had finished. It is important to remember that, even though the cattle barons were better funded and had more weapons, they were not able to defeat the locals of Buffalo, who believed they had the law on their side.

10 Conflict on the Plains

10.1 Conflict between settlers and Plains Indians: the Indian Wars

When white settlers first ventured onto the Plains, they thought it was impossible to live on them. Because of this, the US government agreed treaties with the Indian tribes and created the **Permanent Indian Frontier**, which ran down the 95th parallel, just west of the Mississippi river. All the Indian tribes in the eastern states moved west of this point. However, as the new American civilisation spread west, this brought the two sides into conflict.

The white Americans wanted to settle and farm the land on the Plains. The US government set aside areas of land called **reservations** for the Indians to live on. The Indians were expected to stay and farm on this land but they had no experience of this. They wanted to maintain their ancient way of life of following the buffalo across the Plains.

Key terms

Permanent Indian Frontier – the US government assigned all lands west of the Mississippi river as a permanent Indian domain, in an attempt to relocate all Indians living in the eastern USA.

Reservations – areas of land set aside by the US government for Indians to live on.

Key content

- How differing attitudes created conflict between the Plains Indians and the white settlers
- The events that led to increased tension between the Plains Indians and the white settlers
- Why the Plains Indians and US government ended up at war

How differing attitudes created conflict between the Plains Indians and the white settlers

Revised

If you look back at the comparison of Indian and white beliefs on page 70, you can see how different they were. The main sticking point was the belief about **land:**

- The Plains Indians could not understand the idea of owning land.
- The white settlers thought the Indians were wasting the land, and that they were lazy because they were not farming it.

When the US government originally created the Permanent Indian Frontier of the Plains, they had not wanted any of the land: you will remember that they referred to it as a desert and thought it was useless. But once **gold was discovered** and the idea of **Manifest Destiny** took hold (see page 81), that attitude changed. Now the Indians were just in the way – and wasting all that land!

- As white settlement expanded westwards into formerly Indian land there was inevitable conflict. The white settlers mostly developed a negative attitude towards the Indians. They wanted them dealt with harshly to get them out of the way. In fact, they were nicknamed **exterminators** because they wanted the Indians gone.
- Their views were not shared by the government and population in the east, who had more peaceful ideas. They were nicknamed **negotiators** because they wanted to negotiate settlements with the Indians.

However the white settlers had more influence on relationships because they were actually living on the Plains. In theory the US government could send in the army to defend the Treaty but in practice the army sided with the settlers and the exterminators.

Exam practice

1. Why were the homesteaders and other Plains settlers likely to think like **exterminators**?
   (12 marks)

Answers online

Revision task

List each of the following group's attitudes towards the Indians, and the reasons why they felt this way:

- Exterminators
- Negotiators

The events that led to increased tension between the Plains Indians and the white settlers

Revised ☐

1851: Fort Laramie Treaty

Indian tribes agreed to stop attacking wagon trains on the Oregon Trail in return for permanent control of a long strip of land across the centre of the continent. The US government also promised to protect the Indians.

1862: Little Crow's War

Little Crow was the leader of the Santee Sioux. Due to a crop failure when pests devastated their crops, and a delay in the compensation payments, by August the tribe were starving. They attacked government warehouses, taking the food and burning the buildings, before attacking the soldiers sent to deal with them. But the victory was only temporary. By October the war was over and the Santee Sioux were punished by being moved to a smaller reservation where their problems were made even worse by a lack of clean water.

1864: The Sand Creek Massacre

The Cheyenne, led by Black Kettle, suffered a similar problem to the Santee Sioux from 1861 and began attacking wagon trains in their desperation for food. After three years of attacks, they finally agreed to meet government officials to come to an agreement. Unfortunately, while these talks were going on, the army massacred 450 Indians in a dawn raid on their camp at Sand Creek, although it was festooned with white flags of surrender. This incident led to the Cheyenne giving up their land claims in Colorado in return for land in Oklahoma.

1865: Red Cloud's War

The discovery of gold in Montana led to the Bozeman Trail being set up, so that miners could reach the gold fields. Unfortunately this new trail broke the Fort Laramie Treaty, as it crossed the Sioux hunting lands. **Red Cloud**, chief of the Lakota Sioux, along with Sitting Bull and Crazy Horse, attacked the wagon trains and the army was sent to protect them. The Sioux **adapted** their tactics and fought through the winter. They stopped people using the Bozeman Trail and laid siege to the forts, trapping the army. Eventually the US government had to negotiate a new settlement.

1868: Second Fort Laramie Treaty

Following Red Cloud's War, the government signed a Second Fort Laramie Treaty which created lots of smaller reservations for separate tribes. Red Cloud moved the Lakota Sioux to Dakota territory, around the Black Hills. He believed he had won. However, the smaller reservations brought more change to the way the Indians lived, and further broke down their society.

1874: Discovery of gold in the Black Hills

In 1874 a surveying party discovered huge gold reserves in the Black Hills. The miners moved in, completely ignoring the 1868 Fort Laramie Treaty. The government offered the Sioux money for the land, but no amount of money would have been enough to buy what the Sioux saw as the most sacred land on the continent.

Key term

Red Cloud – a successful war leader of the Sioux until 1868. Afterwards he lived on the reservation, working to expose the corruption of the Indian agent. He died in 1909, aged 90.

Revision task

This page contains a large amount of information! To help you to focus on what is really important, construct a tweet (140 characters or fewer) to summarise each event.

Exam practice

2. Describe the events that led to increased tension between the Indians and the US government in the 1860s. **(9 marks)**

Answers online

Why the Plains Indians and US government ended up at war

Revised

- **Reservations** – The land that was given to the Indians was not good for farming on, and in any case they wanted to continue their way of life of hunting the buffalo across the plains. The US government saw reservations as only a temporary solution.

- **Manifest Destiny** – Perhaps it was a bit short-sighted of the US government to create new reservations. When you remember that Manifest Destiny was about taking over the **whole** continent, it did not leave space for anybody else. Indians were not part of the 'American Dream' by the late nineteenth century.

- **New Indian leaders** – Young warriors like Sitting Bull had witnessed the hardships faced by the Sioux after Little Crow's War, and they could not settle on the new small reservations. They became more popular among the Indians, and they were not prepared to put up with the way they were being treated.

- The second half of the nineteenth century was peppered with attacks by Indians on white settlers and vice versa. Both sides committed horrible acts of violence against their enemies. This led to an increase in tensions and meant the army had to be kept permanently on standby.

Exam practice

3. 'Little Crow's War in 1862 was a victory for the Indians.' Do you agree? Explain your answer. **(16 marks)**

Answers online

Exam tip

When you are constructing your balanced argument for this question, try thinking about it from a short-term and long-term point of view. In the short term, Little Crow won the war; but the long-term impact was not a positive one.

10.2 Conflict between settlers and Plains Indians: the Great Sioux War

While there were many battles between the US army and different Indian tribes, the Great Sioux War was particularly important because it was the last significant victory that the Indians were able to win against the US army. Sioux Indians led by Sitting Bull and Crazy Horse resisted the army's attempts to return them to their reservations. It all came to a head at the Battle of the Little Bighorn. However, as you'll see, what looked like a victory for the Indians was actually to be their downfall.

Key content
- The key events of the Great Sioux War
- The Battle of Little Bighorn
- The key individuals in the Great Sioux War
- How the Plains Indians both won and lost at the Battle of the Little Bighorn

The key events of the Great Sioux War
Revised

- **1874:** General Custer led an expedition into the Black Hills to look for gold. It was quickly discovered.
- **1875:** More than 1000 miners descended on the Black Hills. This broke the Second Fort Laramie Treaty, but neither the army nor the US government took action. The government tried to buy the Black Hills from the Indians, but they rejected the offer.
- **December 1875:** The Sioux were ordered to return to their reservation. They stayed put: roughly 7000 stayed with Sitting Bull and Crazy Horse in Powder River country.
- **February 1876:** The US army began to treat the Sioux as hostile. They began to prepare an attack to force the Sioux back onto the reservation.
- **June 1876:** The attack began, but it did not go well for the US army. It ended in defeat at the Battle of the Little Bighorn
- **4 July 1876:** On Independence Day, news of the defeat reached the east. The public were horrified. 2500 new soldiers were sent west and two new forts were built.
- **Autumn 1876:** The US army attacked bands of the Sioux, gradually reducing their number. The Sioux began to run out of food and ammunition.
- **5 May 1877:** Crazy Horse and his followers surrendered – the last band to do so. This was the end of the armed resistance of the Sioux.

The Battle of Little Bighorn
Revised

- In June 1876, **Sitting Bull** and **Crazy Horse** and 2000 warriors from the Sioux set up camp on the banks of the Bighorn River, an area outside of the Great Sioux Reservation.
- The army began to prepare an attack to force the Sioux back onto the reservation.
- The army planned to trap the Sioux by attacking in three separate columns led by three generals (see diagram 1).

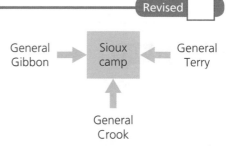

↑ **1 The campaign plan**

Battle of the Rosebud

On 17 June, Crazy Horse and some warriors attacked General Crook's column and killed or injured 90 soldiers before retreating back to camp. Crook's column was severely weakened and could no longer attack the Indian camp.

Changed tactics

Terry and Gibbon joined forces. They changed tactics (see diagram 2).

- The **Seventh Cavalry**, a small but quick force led by **General Custer**, would attack the Sioux camp from the south.
- Custer was offered extra weapons and men but refused them. The larger troop, with more weapons, would attack from the north.

Battle of the Little Bighorn

Custer and his cavalry travelled by day and night to the Sioux camp. As they were smaller and quicker, **they arrived a day earlier** than the larger troop but **were exhausted**. Custer sent out some scouts who reported that the Indians seemed to be packing up to leave camp, so he decided to attack there and then.

- Custer split his small force of 510 men into three groups to attack from different sides.
- Reno's and Benteen's attacks failed and they retreated. They both realised they could not overcome so many Indians.
- Custer carried on. All the Indian warriors were focused on Custer and his small force, now totally outnumbered. They bravely fought on, but all were killed. This was known as **Custer's Last Stand**. Custer and his entire force were killed. Many of his men were scalped or mutilated by the Indians.

Gibbon and Terry

Sioux camp

General Custer

↑ **2 Change of tactics**

Custer: 260 men ALL DIE

Sioux camp

Reno: 125 men RETREAT

Benteen: 125 men RETREAT

↑ **3 The battle**

The key individuals in the Great Sioux War

Revised

Sitting Bull became an important chief of the Sioux after Red Cloud's War (see page 97). He refused to live on the reservation. Together with Crazy Horse, he encouraged roughly 7000 Indians to leave the reservation in protest at the US government's new policy on the Black Hills.

Crazy Horse was a warrior and leader of the Sioux who were refusing to return to the reservation. He began his involvement in the Great Sioux War by attacking one of the columns sent to return the Sioux to their reservation at the Battle of the Rosebud. He then went on to lead his warriors in the Battle of the Little Bighorn. He adjusted his tactics and leadership so that the Indians were fighting a pitched battle. This meant that they were fighting the US military in US military style; and they were very successful.

General Custer was one of several high-ranking military leaders who fought in the Great Sioux War. His troops were the first to arrive at Little Bighorn, thanks to his decision to march through the night straight across the Wolf Mountains. Even though his men were exhausted, and ignoring the advice from his Indian scouts, he chose to attack the Indians camped there without waiting for reinforcements. This meant that his men were severely outnumbered and outgunned by Crazy Horse's forces.

Exam practice

1. Choose **one** of the following and explain his role in the Battle of Little Big Horn.
   - Crazy Horse
   - General Custer

(9 marks)

Answers online

How the Plains Indians both won and lost at the Battle of the Little Bighorn

The Battle of the Little Bighorn was fought on 25 June 1876. It was the final battle of the Great Sioux War. Even though the Indians won this battle, they were so harshly treated by the US government afterwards that it marked the end of their armed resistance to American expansion.

Won	Lost
● Sitting Bull managed to unite 7000 Indians under his leadership from several different tribes. ● Thanks to their history of **adapting to difficult conditions**, the Indians were able to change their battle tactics to suit the enemy they were fighting. ● Crazy Horse's forces wiped out Custer's entire company. They definitely won the Battle of Little Bighorn in military terms.	● The news of the Indian victory reached the east on 4 July 1876 – the hundredth anniversary of the USA's independence. It could not have been worse timing. The Indians lost much of their remaining public support. ● New forts were built and 2500 extra soldiers were sent to hunt and attack the remaining bands of Indians. ● Eventually, starving and without ammunition, all the bands surrendered or escaped to Canada. They were forced to sell the Black Hills and other land. ● They were moved to an even smaller reservation and placed under military rule. ● Their horses and weapons were taken away.

So, even though the Battle of Little Bighorn is also known as Custer's Last Stand, it could also accurately be called the Sioux's Last Stand.

Revision tasks

1. Look back at the other examples of conflict between the Indians and the US army on pages 97–98. Copy and complete the table below. Compare the Sioux War with the other wars. How similar was the conflict? What were the differences?

Conflict	How it was similar to the Sioux War	How it was different from the Sioux War
Little Crow's War		
The Sand Creek Massacre		
Red Cloud's War		

2. Copy and complete the table below to help you work through the issues around the Battle of the Little Bighorn. Use the information about the battle to help you write bullet points under these headings.

The US government		The Indians	
Failure	Success	Failure	Success

Exam practice

2. 'The Battle of the Little Big Horn in 1876 was a victory for the Indians.' Do you agree? Explain your answer. **(16 marks)**

3. 'The discovery of gold was the main reason for the Sioux Wars in the 1860s and 1870s.' Do you agree? Explain your answer. **(16 marks)**

Answers online

Exam tip

Because the Great Sioux War was a short-term victory but a long-term loss for the Sioux, it is really important to get the facts fixed in your head so that you are not confused by a question that asks you if it really was a victory (see exam practice question 2).

10.3 Change of policy from 1876: destruction of the Native American way of life

After the Battle of Little Bighorn, many people who had been sympathetic to the Indians before now turned against them. Support for the **exterminators** grew, and so there was a lot of pressure on the US government to get rid of the Indians permanently. They did this using laws such as the Dawes Act, and using the army to hound the Indians onto reservations. They also encouraged the destruction of the enormous herds of buffalo, which deprived the Indians of their way of life. In a time where everyone was focusing on fulfilling Manifest Destiny, and white people's ideas about non-white races were less enlightened, the US government did not see what it was doing as wrong.

Key content

- Groups who had an impact on the Plains Indians' way of life: the government, the army and the railroads
- The impact of the Dawes Act on the Plains Indians
- Why the Battle of Wounded Knee marked a significant point in Indian affairs

Groups who had an impact on the Plains Indians' way of life: the government, the army and the railroads

Revised ☐

It fought **winter campaigns**, attacking the Indians throughout the coldest months

It used **Indian scouts**

It waged **total war** on the Indians, destroying their homes and belongings so they had to move to reservations

New tactics

It passed the **Dawes Act** (see below)

It came up with the system of **reservations**

It gave away land promised to the Indians at events such as the **Oklahoma Land Grab, 1889**

US army

US government

It built **forts** to use as bases on the Plains

WHO HAD THE BIGGEST IMPACT ON THE INDIANS?

It supported and funded the **army** and encouraged the building of **railroads**

They crossed **traditional hunting grounds**

The railroads

They enabled **soldiers** to move around more quickly

They brought **homesteaders** onto the Plains, and encouraged ranchers to **drive cattle** across them

They ran hunting expeditions which helped to **destroy the buffalo**

Revision tasks

Each one of the three groups named here had an impact on the Indians' way of life. But did some of the actions have a bigger impact than others?

1. Score each action on the concept map out of 10, with 10 being the biggest impact.
2. Then add up the scores.
3. The group with the highest points had the biggest impact.
4. Do you agree with how the scores worked out? Explain why/why not.

Exam practice

1. Choose **one** of the following and explain their role in destroying the Plains Indians' traditional way of life after 1876.

   - The US government
   - The US army   **(9 marks)**

Answers online

Exam tip

Take care over the date here: the examiner is asking you about the impact on the Plains Indians **after** 1876; therefore you should not include anything about the Plains Wars or the earlier treaties.

The impact of the Dawes Act on the Plains Indians

Revised

The key facts of the Dawes General Allotment Act:

● It was passed in 1887.
● It divided Indian reservations into 160-acre parcels – just like the homesteads of the white settlers.
● Adults received 160 acres; children received 80 acres.
● The rest of the land was sold to white settlers.

In practice, many Indians refused the land, or sold it to white settlers for a fraction of what it was worth. This was because many of them did not want to settle into a farming lifestyle. They became even more dependent on handouts from the US government. The Plains Indians are often described as a proud people, and relying on what they thought of as a foreign government further demoralised them.

Exam tip

You might find it difficult to pull together enough information for two or three good paragraphs when answering this question. You can extend your explanation by going back to pages 68–71 and looking at how the Plains Indians lived, and then analysing the Dawes Act to look at exactly how it attacked their way of life.

Exam practice

2. Why did the Dawes Act have such a negative impact on the Plains Indians? **(12 marks)**

Answers online

Why the Battle of Wounded Knee marked a significant point in Indian affairs

Revised

The Battle of Wounded Knee took place at the very end of 1890. The Seventh Cavalry – the same army unit which had fought at Little Bighorn – attacked a large group of Indians at Wounded Knee, on the Sioux reservation.

Life on this reservation had been very bad for a while. The Sioux, without horses, weapons or food, did the only thing they could think of to try and make things better – they asked the spirit world for help. They danced the **Ghost Dance**. Unfortunately this was illegal under reservation law and the Seventh Cavalry moved in to arrest the ringleaders. Sitting Bull was the first victim: he was shot by a Sioux policeman.

Then, on 28 December, a scuffle broke out between the army and the followers of the Ghost Dance, who were led by Big Foot. The Seventh Cavalry opened fire, killing 146 Indians, including seven babies. The bodies were left for three days before being buried in a mass grave.

For the Plains Indians, this marked the end of their resistance. They had tried fighting, negotiating, adapting and, finally, praying. Unfortunately the US government, with its army and strong vision of Manifest Destiny, proved to be too strong an enemy. The Battle of Wounded Knee marked the end of the Indian resistance.

Key term

Ghost Dance – the Ghost Dance movement was founded by a medicine man called Wovoka in 1888. He preached that if Indians remained peaceful and danced the Ghost Dance, a new world would come, in which there were no whites. The buffalo and all the dead Indians would come back to life.

This is a painful and bleak episode in world history. It is important to remember the people involved in the conflict, and to be respectful of their memories.

Exam tip

To answer this question you could also bring in some information from the previous sections. Remember that this marked the very end of the Sioux struggle on the Plains. You could mention, for example, how the destruction of the buffalo meant their old lifestyle was now impossible and how the Dawes Act led to a change in their social structure.

Exam practice

3. Describe what happened at the Battle of Wounded Knee. **(9 marks)**

Answers online

10.4 Changes to Native American culture by 1890: life on reservations

When the Indians first saw the white settlers turn up on the east coast, they could never have imagined that their way of life, which had lasted for centuries, would soon be ended. The arguments over the land and the inability of the Indians and white settlers to live peacefully together meant that, as well as going to war with the Indians, the white government set about making sure their culture was destroyed as well. This would weaken the resistance of the Indians and eventually meant that the US government could stop fighting with the Indians, because there was nobody left who was willing to fight.

Key content

- How life on reservations differed from the traditional Indian way of life
- How the buffalo became almost extinct
- How Indian culture was dismantled by the US government

How life on reservations differed from the traditional Indian way of life

Revised

From 1825, with the Permanent Indian Frontier, the government started requiring Indians to live on specific pieces of land, which over time got smaller and smaller. These were called **reservations**. The Indians had to change their lifestyle in order to adapt to their new conditions.

Traditional life	Reservation life
● **Nomadic**: moved around the Plains. ● Bands were led by chiefs, who were advised by elders on what was best for the band. ● Hunted the buffalo for food (and everything else!). ● Horses were the most important thing an Indian could own. Wealth was measured in horses.	● Lived on one specific area of land. ● Supervised by government-appointed **Indian agents**. These men were often dishonest and cheated the Indians. ● Encouraged to farm the land – even though it was often poor quality. When they could not grow enough food, they relied on government handouts. ● Often forced to live without horses/weapons.

How the buffalo became almost extinct

Revised

There were an estimated 13 million buffalo on the Plains before 1840. However, by 1885, there were only around 200 left. This was as a direct result of white settlements growing on the Plains.

Destruction of habitat – Homesteaders moving to the Plains fenced off large pieces of land which destroyed the natural migration patterns of the buffalo herds. After cattle ranching became popular on the Plains, there was not enough grazing land to support the herds.

Hunting for sport – The **transcontinental railroad** ran excursions for people to shoot the buffalo. In fact, if a train passed by a herd, it would often stop and encourage the passengers to shoot as many buffalo as possible. The railroads also employed hunters to supply buffalo meat to their workers, and keep the buffalo clear of the tracks.

Hunting for hides – After 1871, when a new method of making leather was discovered, buffalo hides became very valuable. The new hunters had high-powered rifles and were very efficient. Bone pickers would wait until the rest of the carcass had rotted and then collect the bones and hooves to sell. With so many people making money from the buffalo, their numbers fell drastically.

Deliberate extermination – Some sources suggest that the US government and army deliberately wiped out as many buffalo as possible. This meant that the Indians had no food source left and were forced to live on reservations and accept government handouts. The army gave free ammunition to buffalo hunters.

Revision tasks

1. Read Source A. What impact did Sheridan think the extinction of the buffalo would have on the Indians?

2. Look back to pages 68–69. Make a list of all the things about their lifestyle the Indians would have to change if they were not able to hunt the buffalo.

Source A: General Philip H. Sheridan in a speech to the Texas legislature in 1873

'These men [the buffalo hunters] have done more in the last two years, and will do more in the next year to settle the vexed Indian question, than the entire regular army has done in the last 30 years. They are destroying the Indians' food supply … Send them powder and lead if you will; but for the sake of a lasting peace, let them kill, skin and sell until the buffalos are exterminated.'

How Indian culture was dismantled by the US government

Revised ☐

- **Territorial:** The US government split up the tribes into smaller groups so that they could not work together. Later on, the Dawes Act allowed Indian farmers to claim their own homesteads, further weakening tribal bonds.

- **Political:** The old system of chiefs did not work in the reservations, where the Indian agent was in charge, helped by the Indian police. The old system of honour and elders was destroyed.

- **Economic:** Without horses and buffalo, the Indians had no system of trade left.

- **Religious:** The old religious ceremonies were banned – and anyway, what was the point of doing a Buffalo Dance if there were no buffalo to hunt? Christian missionaries eventually took over the running of many reservations.

- **Educational:** Indian children were sent to military-style boarding schools where they were not allowed to speak their language, learn their history or follow their beliefs. By destroying an entire generation's sense of nationality, the US government made sure the Indians could never return to their old way of life.

Revision task

Copy and complete the Venn diagram below to show how the Indian culture was eroded. Use the information on this page to help you fill in the circles with the key issues.

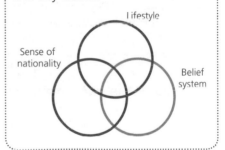

Exam practice

1. Choose **one** of the following and explain their importance in destroying Plains Indian culture.
   - Banning religious ceremonies
   - Educating Indian children in white boarding schools **(9 marks)**

2. Describe the impact reservation life had on the Plains Indians. **(9 marks)**

3. 'The destruction of the buffalo was the main reason for the end of the Plains Indians' traditional way of life'. Do you agree? Explain your answer. **(16 marks)**

Answers online

Exam tip

You can reuse your previous answer for question 2 on page 103 as the counter-argument for question 3: the impact of the Dawes Act is another factor in the end of the Plains Indians' traditional way of life.

11.1 The early years: the Weimar Republic

The First World War ended on 11 November 1918. Soon after this, the old German government, which had been led by the **Kaiser**, was forced out of Germany. It was replaced by a new government called the **Weimar Republic**. This new republic faced serious problems as it was unpopular with many people living in Germany as well as soldiers coming back from the war. Some of the German people blamed the politicians for losing the war because they had signed an **armistice**, and had agreed to terms which seriously weakened Germany's power. The anger towards the Weimar Republic spilled out onto the streets. Soon different groups within Germany began to fight openly with the government. Additionally, the build-up of economic problems led to widespread hunger and poverty which made the Weimar Republic even more unpopular.

Key content

- Problems faced by the leaders of the Weimar Republic
- The creation of the Nazi Party

Problems faced by the leaders of the Weimar Republic

Revised

Problem 1: Blame for defeat in the First World War

When the leaders of the Weimar Republic signed the armistice that ended the fighting, many Germans were shocked. The Kaiser had not told the German people that they were losing the war, and victory seemed possible. They felt betrayed and were looking for someone to blame. The people believed that Germany could have won the war if the army had not been stabbed in the back by the weak politicians who lacked the will to fight on. This was known as the '**stab in the back**' myth.

Problem 2: The Treaty of Versailles

The German people blamed the Weimar Government for signing the Treaty of Versailles. Some of the key terms in the treaty included the following:

- Germany had to give up 13 per cent of its **l**and including **colonies** and important areas with raw materials such as coal.
- The **a**rmy was reduced to 100,000 (it had been 1.75 million); no conscription or aircraft were allowed and there was a reduction in the size of the navy.
- Germany had to pay a huge sum of **m**oney – £6.6 billion – as **reparations** to countries such as France and Belgium which had been devastated by trench warfare.
- The 'war guilt' clause meant that Germany accepted **b**lame for causing the war.

These terms were hard. Opponents of the Weimar Republic saw the government as weak because it had signed the Treaty and agreed to these terms.

Exam tip

For your exam you need to remember the key terms in the Treaty. To remember these, use the acronym **LAMB** (**L** = Land, **A** = Army, **M** = Money, **B** = Blame).

Problem 3: Proportional representation

In the old government, the Kaiser had chosen the ministers who would help him run the country. The new constitution brought in by the Weimar Republic allowed the German people to choose who they wanted in their government. This new system was much fairer as all Germans over the age of 20 could vote and all adults had the right to free speech. The government counted the votes using a system known as **proportional representation (PR)**. While this method seemed fair, it often meant that parliament was made up of lots of different minor parties which had too much influence on policies. The major parties in the **Reichstag** had to make deals with the minor parties because they needed their support.

Problem 4: Political violence

Not all people felt that the way the leaders ran the Weimar Republic was the best way for Germany to be ruled. Many extreme parties wanted to destroy the Republic and its system of government, and seize power to rule Germany their way. The main groups can be split into extreme left-wing and extreme right-wing parties:

Extreme left wing   **Extreme right wing**

The Spartacist Rising, 1919	The Kapp Putsch, 1920
The members of the Spartacist League were **communists** who wanted a revolution in Germany. The government ordered the army and the **Freikorps** to crush them. Leaders were executed for their part in the rising.	The leader of the Freikorps, Wolfgang Kapp, attempted to seize power using the Freikorps. Workers went on a general strike to protest, and managed to stop this uprising.
The Red Rising, 1920	**The Munich Putsch, 1923**
A communist army of around 50,000 workers occupied the Ruhr. The army and the Freikorps crushed them with a loss of around 1000 communists.	Adolf Hitler's Nazi Party of around 50,000 members and their own private army (the **SA**) wanted to seize power. Their plan was to take over the government and set up a new one in Munich. Poor planning meant it failed and Hitler and the other Nazi leaders were arrested and sent to prison.

Revision task

Create your own memory map showing 'problems faced by the leaders of the Weimar Republic 1918–23'. Use the information on pages 106–107 to add branches for:

- Blame for defeat in the First World War
- The Treaty of Versailles
- Proportional representation
- Political violence

Source A: A cartoon with the title 'Clemenceau the Vampire', 1919, printed in the German newspaper *Kladderadatsch*. Clemenceau was the leader of France who had made sure the Treaty of Versailles was harsh on Germany

Exam tip

The first question on the exam paper nearly always start with a simple source question such as 'What can you learn from Source A ...'.

You don't just describe the source or copy it out. You need to go beyond what you see in the source, to use your background knowledge to explain it.

Some of the most common kinds of sources used in this question are cartoons. Cartoons usually contain a strong message so try to work out what this message is by using the clues in the source and your knowledge.

How to answer this question:

1. **Look.** Examine the source closely – what can you see? You could write annotations around the source so that you don't miss anything. *What can you see in Source A? Who are the people? What are they doing? What are the items next to the bed? What does this tell us about the woman? What does the caption tell us?*

2. **Infer.** Use your background knowledge to explain what you can see. Why has the artist/writer put this detail in? What can you work out from the source and your knowledge about their beliefs? *How did the German people react to the Treaty of Versailles? What did they think of Clemenceau?*

3. **Write.** Then you are ready to write about the source. Include examples from the source that back up what you are saying. *In Source A, you can see a vampire is sucking the blood of an innocent women. The caption says that the vampire is Clemenceau, the French president. Your inference could be that the Treaty of Versailles, led by France (the vampire), is draining Germany (the woman) of its power.*

4. **Look back** and check you have answered the question. For 4 marks, you need to write and infer about two things you can see in the source, supporting your inferences with background knowledge.

Exam tip

For the 'describe' question, you need to describe two to three points
and provide supporting evidence to back up each point that you
make. Choose information that is relevant to the question.

Here you should focus on how the Treaty of Versailles had a
damaging effect on the German people. Use connecting words
such as 'As well as this', 'Additionally', 'This meant that', to link and
develop your points.

Make sure you read what the question is asking you to describe
before you start writing. After you have written a response, read it
again to check you have covered everything.

The creation of the Nazi Party

Revised ☐

Hitler becomes leader of the Nazis

- **1918:** Hitler had been a soldier in the trenches during the First
  World War. While he was in hospital recovering from a gas attack,
  the German government surrendered. Like many Germans, Hitler felt
  betrayed and angry as a result.

- **1919:** When he went back to Germany, Hitler was asked by the
  army to spy on some extremist groups. While attending a meeting
  of one of these groups, the German Workers' Party, he was so
  impressed that he joined. At this time it was a newly formed party,
  with only 55 members.

- **1920:** Hitler had become more involved with the party. He was able
  to rename it the National Socialist German Workers' Party (Nazis).

  They believed that democracy only led to weak government. They
  thought that there should be only one political party, with one
  leader. Hitler declared a Twenty-Five Point programme outlining their
  beliefs.

- **1921:** Hitler began to show his natural ability to speak well in public.
  In 1921 he eventually challenged and succeeded in becoming the
  leader of the party.

- **1923:** The Nazis had 55,000 members, but they were still seen as a
  marginal political party.

↑ **Adolf Hitler**

Points from the Twenty-Five Point programme, 1920

- Unite all German-speaking people.
- Abolish the Treaty of Versailles and end reparations.
- Share all profits made by profiteers during the war.
- Form a strong central government with unrestricted authority.
- Take over land and colonies in Eastern Europe to feed Germany's
  population.

Exam tip

A good way to remember these
points is to think of them as

Unite

Abolish

Profit

Strong

Land.

Revision task

Make up your own mnemonic to remember the points using
the letters **U, A, P, S** and **L**, for example **U**ncle's **A**pple **P**ie **S**mells
Lovely.

11.2 Challenges and recovery: the impact of economic problems 1923–29

In 1923 the Weimar Republic faced an economic crisis that nearly brought the country to its knees. It all started when Germany missed a reparations payment in 1922. This set off a series of events that led to **hyper-inflation** and economic chaos. Amid this chaos, Hitler and the Nazis tried (but failed) to seize power.

The economic problems almost destroyed the Weimar Government but a new leader, Stresemann, took some bold decisions that helped the government to survive. In fact the period 1924–29 has been referred to as the 'Golden Years' as Germany became much more stable and prosperous.

> ### Key content
> - Why 1923 was such a crucial year
> - Stresemann and the recovery of Germany, 1924–29

Revised

Why 1923 was such a crucial year

Hyper-inflation

> **1922**: Germany missed a reparations payment.

> **1923**: French and Belgian troops responded by invading the Ruhr to take what was owed to them in the form of raw materials and goods. The Weimar Republic told the workers not to co-operate with the invaders and to go on strike using **passive resistance**. Unfortunately the German government still paid the workers' families and slowly ran out of money. Its solution was to print more money but this led to further problems.

> As the government printed more money to pay its workers the money reduced in value. Shops and suppliers put up prices, and so people had to be paid more. Soon it spiralled out of control and led to hyper-inflation. Everyday goods such as food items like eggs and bread became unaffordable. Not everyone was affected badly by the crisis, yet most people in Germany suffered during this time and life was very difficult. Here are some of the results of hyper-inflation.

People with loans found it easier to pay back their debts as their loans were worth much less than they had been.	Those with fixed incomes suffered such as some workers and pensioners. Even the increases that some workers had could not match the rise in prices.
Anybody with savings watched them reduce in value and become worthless.	People lost confidence in the government as it was seen to be powerless over hyper-inflation. This led to more people turning to extremist parties instead.
Some businessmen were able to pay back loans used to set up their companies.	
People had died during the crisis in the Ruhr.	

> = The problems of hyper-inflation turned many people against the government. An opportunity for the Nazis!

Key term

Hyper-inflation – inflation is when prices increase, so more money is needed to pay for the same things; hyper-inflation is where this gets completely out of hand and prices rise enormously.

Key term

Passive resistance – opposing government action in non-violent ways, refusing to co-operate, staging strikes, etc.

Revision task

Hyper-inflation affected the German people in different ways. Draw a set of scales under the title 'Hyper-inflation'. Write the negative effects of hyper-inflation on one side and the positive effects on the other side. Which side has the most points?

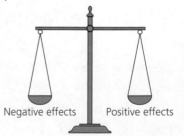

Negative effects   Positive effects

The Munich Putsch

With the German economy in turmoil, Hitler saw his opportunity to overthrow the Weimar Republic and begin his revolution. He had managed to trick the former army leader General Ludendorff into allowing him use of his troops.

- Hitler and 600 SA members interrupted a meeting of the Bavarian government in a beer hall. He announced he was going to overthrow the government.

- The next day, around 3000 Nazis, including Hitler, marched through Munich. The police broke up the march and Hitler was arrested.

The Munich Putsch was a failure in the short term. But in the longer term, it was a success for the Nazis.

- Hitler's trial was publicised all around Germany which made him a household name.

- He was sentenced to five years in prison but only served nine months!

- While in prison he wrote a book called *Mein Kampf* which set out his key beliefs and how he wanted to achieve them.

Stresemann and the recovery of Germany, 1924–29

Revised ☐

Stresemann was a key individual in the 'Golden Years' of 1924–29, yet how successful were the reforms he introduced?

One of Stresemann's first actions was to sort out **hyper-inflation**. He succeeded in this by recalling the old currency and replacing it with a new one called the Rentenmark. Inflation was quickly brought under control.

→ *However*, many people in Germany had lost savings during this time and so could not forget how hyper-inflation had affected them.

In 1924 he negotiated the **Dawes Plan** which gave Germany longer to pay off its reparations and brought in more US loans. The government used the money to build new infrastructure such as railways and factories.

→ *However*, some people say the loans made Germany too dependent on the US economy.

By signing the **Locarno Treaties** in 1925 with countries such as Britain, France and Belgium, Stresemann improved relationships with these countries. By joining the **League of Nations** in 1926, Germany became involved in major decisions internationally.

→ *However*, in his own country some Germans felt Stresemann had not done enough and should have won back the land lost with the Treaty of Versailles.

Stresemann successfully negotiated the **Young Plan** in 1929 which gave Germany even more time to pay off the reparations.

→ *However*, this did not please some people in the country. Some felt they should not be paying the reparations at all and this only meant extending the time they would be paying them for!

Exam practice

1. 'Stresemann was a strong and popular leader who ensured Germany became a stable and prosperous country in the years 1923–29.' Do you agree? Explain your answer. **(16 marks)**

Answers online

Exam tip

The 'do you agree' question comes at the end of your exam paper and is worth the most marks. You need to write a balanced answer.

Questions like this that ask you for your opinion about a statement require you to give a balanced answer. Imagine you are in a courtroom and you need to listen to the prosecution and the defence lawyers' views first before the judge makes an overall decision.

- What evidence would you use to support the claim in the statement?

- What evidence would you use to argue against the claim in the statement?

- Finally, write your overall conclusion. Which side of the argument has the strongest claim? Write down your opinion and explain why you have come to this conclusion.

11.3 Increasing support for the Nazi Party

In 1923, the Nazi Party failed in their attempt to take control of Germany (see page 107). The immediate results of the Munich Putsch were Adolf Hitler's imprisonment and the Nazi Party being banned from politics. But instead of this being the end, the Nazi Party emerged from the crisis reorganised and ready to convince the citizens of Germany that they were serious contenders to lead the country.

(see page 107)

Key content

- How the Nazis tried to gain support before 1928
- Reasons why the Nazis did not succeed in gaining power by 1928
- Reasons for the dramatic increase in support for the Nazis after 1929

How the Nazis tried to gain support before 1928

Revised

- **Change of tactics** – The Munich Putsch showed Hitler and the Nazi Party that trying to take over control of Germany by force was not going to work. Instead, they realised their route to power lay in **being elected** by the people.

- **The appeal of ideas** – Even though Hitler went to jail for masterminding the Munich Putsch, some of his **ideas** did appeal to those in Germany who resented the Treaty of Versailles. Yet it was **his way of delivering these ideas** that was his strength. Hitler was a brilliant speaker and his speeches excited audiences.

- **The role of propaganda** – Joseph Goebbels was in charge of persuading the German people that the Nazi Party were serious contenders to run the country. He used **propaganda** methods such as posters, political meetings and newspapers to deliver the Nazi message and increase their support.

- **The work of the SA** – The SA was set up in 1921 by Hitler to stop Nazi meetings being interrupted by followers of other parties. However, the SA were more likely to disrupt the meetings of their opponents. They often used **violence and intimidation**. Some Germans were put off by their violence, but others praised the SA for their organisation.

- **Nazi organisations** – The Nazis wanted to increase support for the party among different groups in Germany. They did this by creating organisations such as the **Hitler Youth** and the League of German Maidens.

Key term

Propaganda – passing information to people to try to deliberately influence or persuade them in some way.

Revision task

Using the information on this page, study the statements below and decide whether they are true or false. When you have identified which are false, rewrite them so they are true.

Statement	True/false
a. The Munich Putsch showed Hitler that using force was the best way to gain power.	
b. Joseph Goebbels used propaganda such as posters and newspapers to persuade the German people to vote for the Nazis.	
c. Hitler was a poor speaker and often bored people in the audience.	
d. The SA were used to disrupt meetings of other political opponents.	
e. During this period the Nazis decided not to create organisations such as the Hitler Youth.	

Reasons why the Nazis did not succeed in gaining power by 1928

Revised

Despite the changes made by the Nazis during the 1920s to try to increase support for the party, the results of the 1928 election showed that only 3 per cent of Germans had actually voted for them.

There are a number of reasons why the Nazis had not succeeded in gaining power by the 1928 election:

- **They lacked the support of the working class:** The Nazis had failed to gain the support of the majority of the working class, who preferred other parties such as the Social Democratic Party or the Communist Party.
- **Hitler was banned from speaking:** Hitler was banned from public speaking until 1928 so was unable to use his skills as an orator to persuade Germans.
- **1924–28 was a time of prosperity:** Stresemann's economic and political policies had been successful. Unemployment was low and Germany had built up positive relationships with other countries.
- **Nazi ideas were too extreme:** Some of the ideas and beliefs of the Nazis, such as anti-Semitic ideas, invading other countries and using violence as a form of control, were too extreme. This put many people off.

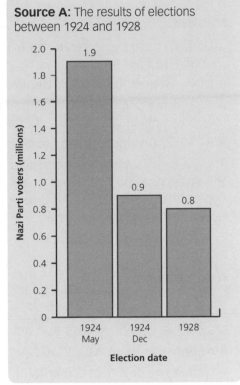

Source A: The results of elections between 1924 and 1928

Nazi Parti voters (millions) / Election date

1924 May: 1.9
1924 Dec: 0.9
1928: 0.8

Exam practice

1. Explain the reasons why the Nazis had failed to get into power by 1928. **(9 marks)**

Answers online

Exam tip

Questions like this require you to explain how something happened. Try not to describe in story form why the Nazis did not get into power. Instead list the reasons why they failed and explain each reason in detail. Use the information above to help you answer this question.

Reasons for the dramatic increase in support for the Nazis after 1929

Revised

From 1929 onwards the Nazis' fortunes improved dramatically.

- In the 1930 election the Nazis' had their first breakthrough. They won 18 per cent of the vote and got 107 seats in the Reichstag.
- In July 1932 they won 37 per cent of the vote and 207 seats. They were now the largest political party. They did not have an overall majority so Hitler did not become Chancellor – yet (you will find out how that happened on page 115).

This was a remarkable turnaround for a party that did so badly in 1928 and it needs explaining.

Revision task

This is a favourite topic for exam questions so make sure you know the factors on pages 114–115 well and know how they contributed to Nazi success. Create a revision card for each factor. On one side write the heading, on the other the key points. Include a card for 'political deal'. If you can add examples to each card from your course even better.

Effects of the Wall Street Crash and the Great Depression

The German economy was dependent on loans from America. In 1929, the American stock market, known as 'Wall Street', crashed. It led to a worldwide economic collapse and the period of history known as the Great Depression. This soon affected Germany.

- US banks started to **recall their loans**. German companies were unable to pay.
- Many German firms went **bankrupt**. Millions lost their jobs.
- With more unemployment came **less demand** for food and goods, sinking Germany deeper into depression.
- By 1932, **unemployment** in Germany had **reached 6 million**.

The Weimar Government appeared to stumble aimlessly through this crisis, not knowing what to do. It was scared of a repeat of the hyper-inflation of 1923, so did not want to spend money it did not have on solving unemployment.

This helped the Nazi Party because …

The German people blamed the Weimar Republic for the Great Depression and for high unemployment, and became less supportive as unemployment and poverty grew. They started to turn to more extremist political parties, such as the Nazis.

Nazi promises

Hitler and the Nazis promised to:

- solve the economic crisis and get people back to work
- destroy the Treaty of Versailles
- restore the power of the army
- make Germany powerful again
- be strong leaders of the country.

These were almost exactly the same things they had been saying in the 1920s. The difference was that the chaos and despair of the depression years meant that many ordinary Germans had lost faith in democratic political parties. German people now wanted to hear these messages.

Fear of communism

As their lives became more difficult, more workers started to support the Communist Party. However, this terrified many German businessmen and farmers, because they had seen communism in action in the Soviet Union where the government had taken over land and wealth from big industries and farmers.

The middle class, the businessmen and the farmers didn't want the Communist Party to get into power, so they turned to the Nazis because of their anti-communist stance. Rich businessmen gave them money for campaigning.

Hitler's leadership

Hitler was a charismatic and influential public speaker who was able to get across Nazi ideas and make the German people believe what he was saying. He was also surrounded by a team of very loyal and effective leaders.

Hitler's speeches gained a great deal of support for the Nazis.

Nazi propaganda

- Joseph Goebbels was in charge of Nazi propaganda. He used the **latest technology** – film, loudspeakers and slide shows.
- In 1932, Hitler **travelled around Germany by plane** so that he could talk to as many people as possible.
- **Mass rallies** made people feel proud to be German and added a sense of order and discipline.
- **Posters** were used effectively to spread Nazi ideas.

This propaganda got the Nazi message across to people very effectively. It increased support for the Nazis.

Local organisations

By 1929, the Nazis had well over 100,000 members, and local parties all over Germany. They were well organised.

- Local leaders ran **public meetings**. The Nazi Party provided carefully trained speakers.
- Local parties **helped the unemployed** by providing soup kitchens and shelters or recruiting them into the local SA.
- The **Hitler Youth** (see page 125) from 1922 provided activities.
- The SA even gained a reputation for being **disciplined young men** (not the threatening thugs of the 1920s).

Weak opposition

There were two natural opponents to the Nazis: the Social Democrats (who were the largest party) and the Communists.

- Neither party took the Nazis seriously and were more concerned with battling each other.
- Voters did not trust the Social Democrats (the ruling party) because they didn't seem to know what to do.

Political problems

- The most successful Weimar politician of the 1920s, Stresemann, died of a stroke in 1929, just days before the Wall Street Crash.
- The democratic ideals of the Weimar constitution caused problems. No party had a majority and there was a series of weak, short-lived governments.
- Some of the measures taken by the government actually made the depression worse. For example it cut pay and benefits for government employees, leading to poverty.
- Because of the weak government, President Hindenberg used Article 48 of the constitution to rule by decree (without getting laws approved by the Reichstag).

The political deal

Following the June 1932 elections, the Nazis were the largest party in the Reichstag, but they did not have an overall majority. No other party wanted to work with them. President Hindenburg had to appoint a Chancellor. He did not want Hitler so he appointed his friend von Papen. But the Reichstag did not support von Papen!

So the result was **stalemate**, and another election in November 1932. The Nazis lost seats but were still the biggest party. This time Hitler did a deal with von Papen, who persuaded Hindenberg to appoint Hitler as Chancellor and himself as Vice Chancellor. Von Papen thought he could control Hitler. How wrong he was!

This helped the Nazi Party because ...

At a time when the national government seemed incompetent or ineffective these local measures impressed many ordinary Germans and increased support for the Nazis. The apparent discipline of the SA was attractive when there was so much violence around the election meetings of 1930 and 1932 – even though the SA often stirred up the violence in the first place!

Weak opposition meant that the Nazis' policies were not challenged or questioned. The opposition offered nothing new while the Nazis did.

The weak government made the Nazi message of strong government more attractive. In fact some people say that Hindenberg's ruling by decree had ended democracy in the Weimar Republic already. And remember some people had never forgiven the Weimar Government for the Treaty of Versailles, the 'stab in the back', reparations and hyper-inflation.

12 Government of the Third Reich

12.1 Creation of the Nazi state

The Wall Street Crash was a hidden blessing for Hitler. A series of chancellors tried, but failed, to solve the problems of the depression.

Hitler eventually became Chancellor in January 1933 and within eighteen months had successfully become **Führer** (Supreme Leader) of Germany. He banned all other political parties and removed any opposition to the Nazis. Hitler changed Germany from a democracy into a dictatorship.

Key term

Führer – the German word for leader.

Key content

- How Hitler became Chancellor in 1933
- How Hitler became *Führer* in 1934

How Hitler became Chancellor in 1933

Revised

Key events:

- Between 1930 and 1932, Chancellor Brüning **failed to solve the economic crisis** brought on by the Wall Street Crash and so was eventually sacked.
- **Election of July 1932** – The Nazis won 230 seats which made them the largest party in the Reichstag, but they did not have complete control. Hindenburg made von Papen the new Chancellor of Germany.
- **Election of November 1932** – Von Papen did not have the support of the Reichstag and so called another election to try to gain more seats for his party. He failed and he still could not get a majority. The Nazis lost seats but were still the biggest party.
- **Hindenburg appointed another Chancellor, Von Schleicher** – He was weak and a poor leader who did not like the democratic system. He only lasted a few months.
- **Hitler became Chancellor** – Von Papen persuaded Hindenburg to make Hitler Chancellor and von Papen Vice Chancellor. On 30 January 1933, Hitler was made Chancellor of Germany. Von Papen thought he could control Hitler, but this was a terrible mistake!

Exam tip

You don't need to know all the details about the political deal. However, you should remember that, in the end, Hitler and the Nazis were granted power by just the kind of political dealing and compromise they so despised. It shows how the Weimar Constitution, so democratic in theory, actually made effective government quite hard, particularly in a time of crisis.

How Hitler became *Führer* in 1934

Revised

Hitler was Chancellor, but he was still in a vulnerable position. At any time President Hindenburg could sack him. Furthermore, support for the Nazi Party was falling.

On page 117 are the seven steps taken by Hitler to secure his position and move from being Chancellor to being dictator of Germany.

Revision task

The information on page 117 is important to learn. Draw your own timeline of the period 1933–34. This should include the seven steps that led to Hitler becoming the Supreme Leader of Germany.

1933

STEP 1: The Reichstag Fire (27 February)	Germany's parliament building – the Reichstag – was burnt down. A Dutch communist called Van Der Lubbe was arrested at the scene. Although he appeared to have acted alone, Hitler was able to use this incident to persuade President Hindenburg to grant him emergency powers. With these powers, Hitler set about arresting and detaining communists and other groups who opposed the Nazis.
STEP 2: New elections (5 March)	This was the third election to be held in Germany in nine months! Hitler used the SA to attack opponents and the Nazis delivered their anti-communist message through propaganda methods such as radio broadcasts. Even though the Nazis achieved their best ever results with 288 seats, it is important to remember that 22 million Germans did not vote for them – they only achieved 52 per cent of the vote.
STEP 3: The Enabling Act (24 March)	This Act was the end of democracy in Germany. The Communist Party were expelled from the Reichstag and could not vote. Without the communists voting, the Act was easily passed by the government. It gave Hitler the power to pass laws without the need to get permission from the Reichstag or President Hindenburg.
STEP 4: Political parties and trade unions banned (May–July)	Hitler continued to remove any element of opposition by getting rid of trade unions in May and then in July banning all new political parties. With the Communist Party and Social Democratic Party already banned, Hitler had successfully created a one-party state in Germany.

1934

STEP 5: The Night of the Long Knives (29–30 June)	Ernst Röhm and 400 other SA leaders were killed on Hitler's orders. Hitler had been worried that their power was beginning to rival his and they were in a position to overthrow him. Röhm had become demanding and wanted to merge the SA with the army, making them more powerful. Army leaders did not like Röhm and demanded Hitler take action. On 30 June, Röhm was murdered while on holiday. Because of this, the army no longer felt threatened.
STEP 6: Death of Hindenburg (2 August)	When Hindenburg died, Hitler combined the position of Chancellor and President making him *Führer* (Supreme Leader) of Germany.
STEP 7: Oath of the army (August)	The final piece in the jigsaw occurred when the army swore their allegiance to Hitler and accepted him as their Supreme Leader and promised to obey him.

Exam practice

1. In what ways did the Reichstag Fire in February 1933 help Hitler increase his control over Germany? **(12 marks)**

Answers online

Exam tip

You need to be careful with this type of question. We call it an 'iceberg question' because, like an iceberg, there is more to it than meets the eye! It only mentions the Reichstag Fire, but you have to analyse the other events that also helped Hitler increase his control over Germany.

1. Answer the part of the question that you can see: how the Reichstag Fire helped Hitler increase his control over Germany.

2. Add other events that were important, such as the Enabling Act and the Night of the Long Knives.

3. Write your conclusion. Compare the events and think about how far they increased Hitler's control over Germany.

12.2 Nazi methods of control

Once Hitler had secured power over Germany, he had to ensure the country and its people stayed loyal to him. Hitler relied on two methods to control the German people: terror and propaganda. Many Germans fell in line with the Nazis, including important groups such as the churches and the courts.

Key content

- Nazi control – terror
- Nazi control – propaganda
- Other groups that were controlled by the Nazis

Nazi control – terror

Revised ☐

Key individual: Himmler, head of all police in Nazi Germany, controlled the German people by terror.

Aim: To scare the German people into following the Nazi message.

The SS: Short for *Schutzstaffel* (protection squad), these fanatical Nazis were Hitler's personal bodyguard. They could arrest people without trial and search their houses. They hunted down any opposition to Nazi rule and ruthlessly destroyed it. The SS had two subdivisions:
- The *Waffen SS* were elite soldiers who followed the regular German army into battle.
- The Death's Head Unit were responsible for running the concentration camps.

The Gestapo: These were the Nazi secret police and they kept a watch on the citizens of Germany. They used methods such as phone tapping and collecting information from informants. Anybody seen to be anti-Nazi was targeted and could be imprisoned, tortured or even sent to a concentration camp without trial.

Concentration camps: The first camps were set up after the Nazis got into power to hold political opponents of the party. These camps only held prisoners for a short period of time. The prisoners were questioned, tortured or forced to work.

By the late 1930s the camps had evolved into much more deadly places. The SS Death's Head Unit forced prisoners to work for Nazi-owned businesses making goods such as weapons. The concentration camps now housed a more diverse mix of prisoners including Jews, communists and whoever else dared criticise the Nazis.

The police: Under the Nazis, the police continued with their normal routines. The difference was that the Nazis controlled them. Many high-ranking policemen were Nazis and so the police spent much of the time helping informants and ignored crimes committed by the Nazis.

TERROR

Local wardens: Each town was divided into blocks, and each block had a warden who would write reports on the people who lived there. They would watch out for people who did not seem to participate in pro-Nazi celebrations. Their reports would go to the Gestapo and could decide whether a person got a job or was arrested for being anti-Nazi.

The courts: All judges had to take the pledge of loyalty to Hitler and become Nazi Party members. This made having a fair trial impossible. New Nazi laws, often punishable by death, were enforced.

Revision task

Summarise the information above in your own mind map to show the different ways the Nazis used terror to control people.

Exam practice

1. Describe how the Nazis used terror to control the German people. **(9 marks)**

Answers online

Exam tip

With 'describe' questions such as this one, it is not asking you to list everything you know. Instead, carefully select four or five factors and then explain them.

Revised

Key individual: Goebbels was put in charge of Nazi propaganda.

Aim: To persuade the German people to follow the Nazi message.

Radio: Radio stations came under the control of the Nazis who were able to decide what should be broadcast. Speeches by Hitler were broadcast while other programmes were censored. The Nazis also mass produced radios and sold them cheaply in order to get their message across to the masses. By 1939, 70 per cent of Germans owned a radio.

Films: Feature films were strictly controlled by the Nazis. Major propaganda films were specifically made by the Nazis to show their views, including the **anti-Semitic** movie *The Eternal Jew.*

Books: When the Nazis came to power, they immediately began destroying books they felt were anti-Nazi, such as those written by Jews or communists. They did this by organising mass book burnings. Any new book that was published had to be censored by the Ministry of Propaganda run by Goebbels.

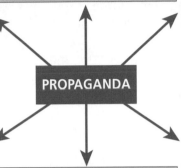

PROPAGANDA

Newspapers: Goebbels closed down any newspapers that did not support the Nazis. He controlled what was printed by sending out daily instructions telling them what stories to include and what angle the writers should take. He also banned Jews from working in or owning a newspaper.

Rallies: The Nazis organised special events to demonstrate to the people and the world how organised and controlled they were. They were often held in huge stadiums and around 100,000 people were involved. The Germans also hosted the Berlin Olympics in 1936 in which Germany won most of the medals. The event was filmed and shown all round the country.

Posters: Anti-Semitic images and images of Hitler and Aryan families (see page 127) were displayed in towns and cities all over Germany. Their purpose was to pass on Nazi messages to as many people as possible.

Revision task

Summarise the information above in your own mind map to show the different ways the Nazis used propaganda to control people.

Key term

Anti-Semitic – suspicion of and hatred of Jews.

Source A: A Nazi poster from the 1930s. The caption reads 'All of Germany hears the Führer on the people's radio'

The radio is seen as a large glowing image in the middle of the crowd. This suggests that the radio was a powerful way the Nazis could get their message across.

The audience is crowded around the radio in the middle of poster. This suggests …

Exam practice

2. What can you learn from Source A about methods used by the Nazis to spread their ideas? **(4 marks)**

Answers online

Exam tip

This type of question is about using your background knowledge to explain a source. Look back at page 108 to see the steps you can take to answer this question.

One inference has been made for you. Identify another one using the sentence starter, and then write your answer to the question.

Other groups that were controlled by the Nazis

The Church

Germany was a religious country with almost 30 per cent of the people belonging to the Catholic Church and 60 per cent to the Protestant Church. The Nazis were opposed to the Christian Church and thought it was a threat to Nazi power. However, they did strike deals with the churches in exchange for their support.

- The Catholic Church and Hitler signed an agreement (the **Concordat**) – the Catholic Church would not interfere in politics and the Nazis would leave the Catholic Church alone.

- The Protestant Church was brought under Nazi control. The '**Reich Church**' was set up and pastors had to swear loyalty to Hitler. Those who objected to this Nazi interference joined the '**Confessional Church**' which was set up outside of Nazi control. There was also the Faith Movement which was the Nazis' 'pagan' alternative to Christianity.

- Some church leaders were intimidated and some, such as Martin Niemöller, were sent to concentration camps for opposing Nazi ideas. Mostly these measures worked to control the churches.

> **Key terms**
>
> **Concordat** – a formal agreement. In this case between the Catholic Church and the Nazi Party.
>
> **Reich Church** – set up and controlled by the Nazis. Pastors had to swear an oath of loyalty to Hitler.
>
> **Confessional Church** – set up by Martin Niemöller to oppose Nazism. He was sent to a concentration camp in 1938.

Exam practice

3. The bullets below show two measures taken by the Nazi regime. Choose one and explain how it helped the Nazis to control Germany.

   - The Nuremberg Rallies
   - The Concordat with the Catholic Church   **(9 marks)**

Answers online

Exam tip

This question is not asking you to connect these two things, you are choosing one only. You must stick to the focus of the question – how this helped the Nazis control Germany. Don't just say it was important, provide evidence to support your point.

12.3 Opposition and resistance to the Nazi government

Many different groups within German society opposed the Nazis and attempted, in their own way, to fight back against the oppression. Opposition to the Nazi regime increased once the war started going badly for Germany after 1941. However, no group succeeded in toppling the regime.

Key content
- The extent to which different groups opposed the Nazis

The extent to which different groups opposed the Nazis

Revised ☐

Opposition Group 1: Former political prisoners 1933–35

Who were they? Leaders and supporters of former opposition parties, including the Communist Party, the Socialist Party and the trade unions. They were large in number and spread out throughout Germany.

Aims and methods These groups were directly opposed to the Nazis and wanted things such as free speech and democracy in Germany. They held secret meetings, organised strikes and handed out leaflets.

How did the Nazis deal with them? At first Hitler was able to control them with the Enabling Act. Later on, many of them were prisoners in concentration camps and those who were left continued their activities in secret.

Opposition Group 2: Edelweiss Pirates 1938–44

Who were they? Gangs of mainly working-class youths from different cities around Germany. They opposed Nazism and the war.

Aims and methods They believed in freedom and saw the Nazi regime as the enemy. Group members used to meet up and play music, go on walks and hand out leaflets in towns. Some of the group used to actively hunt down members of the Hitler Youth and beat them up.

How did the Nazis deal with them? Many were sent to concentration camps or prison. In 1944, around twelve members of the group were hanged by the Nazis for their actions.

Opposition Group 3: The White Rose Group 1942–43

Who were they? A small group of university students lead by Sophie Scholl, Hans Scholl and Christoph Probst.

Aims and methods They believed in justice and wanted to make the German people aware of the atrocities carried out by the regime against minority groups such as the Jews. They spread anti-Nazi messages by handing out leaflets and writing graffiti.

How did the Nazis deal with them? After being spotted by a Nazi informer handing out anti-government leaflets, Hans and Sophie were arrested, tortured and then executed. The group disbanded.

Opposition Group 4: The Confessional Church 1933–45

Who were they? Members of the Protestant Church who had broken away from the 'Reich Church' to form their own Confessional Church.

Aims and methods Martin Niemöller helped set up the Confessional Church to oppose Nazism. He spoke out against policies such as the anti-Semitic laws introduced by Hitler. Dietrich Bonhöffer, another founding member of the Confessional Church, believed that Nazism was anti-religious. He taught ministers that it was evil and should be opposed.

How did the Nazis deal with them? Niemöller was arrested and sent to a concentration camp where he survived the war. He was released when the Allies liberated the camp in 1945. Bonhöffer was also arrested and sent to a concentration camp. He was executed by the SS in 1945.

Opposition Group 5: Army officers – the July Bomb Plot 1944

Who were they? A group of upper-class army officers, the most famous being Claus von Stauffenberg.

Aims and methods Many of the officers opposed the brutal methods used by the SS, especially on the Eastern Front during Hitler's unsuccessful invasion of the USSR. Von Stauffenberg hatched a plan known as Operation Valkyrie which involved assassinating Hitler using a bomb planted in a briefcase. It went off but it failed to kill Hitler.

How did the Nazis deal with them? Hitler reacted ferociously to an attempt on his life. His known opponents, around 5000 people including von Stauffenberg, were arrested and executed.

Revision task

Use the information from pages 121–122 to add supporting evidence for each of the following statements. For example, for statement 3 you may write that members of the White Rose Group handed out leaflets.

1. The Nazis used violence as a punishment to suppress opposition to them.
2. The Nazis used brutal methods of punishment to squash any opposition.
3. Some opposition groups publicly criticised the Nazis.
4. Some opposition groups were active for long periods of Nazi rule.

Exam practice

1. 'Opposition to the Nazis was weak and was not seen as a threat to their power.' Do you agree? Explain your answer. **(16 marks)**

Answers online

Exam tip

Remind yourself of the exam advice on page 111.

For this exam practice question, consider evidence that opposition groups did pose a threat to the Nazis then evidence that shows opposition was weak.

Finally come to a judgement, 'Overall I agree/disagree with this statement because …'

13 Social impact of the Nazi state

13.1 Nazi policies towards women and the young

During the 1920s, women and young people in Germany enjoyed a certain degree of freedom in their lives. Women could choose a career and wear what they liked, and young people were free to choose their own leisure activities outside of school.

This changed when the Nazis came to power. Laws and propaganda changed the lives of women and young people in Germany. Women were told to be mothers and housewives, and the Hitler Youth and the school curriculum trained girls and boys for traditional roles and turned them into loyal Nazis.

Key content

- Nazi policies towards women
- Nazi policies towards young people
- How the war affected policies towards women and young people

Nazi policies towards women

Revised ☐

What the Nazis wanted

- Women to stay at home and have children, while the men went out to work. The role of women revolved around the 'Three Ks': **K**inder, **K**irche, **K**üche (children, church, kitchen).
- Women to wear simple traditional clothes and no high heels or make-up.
- Women to be strong and healthy to help with child bearing – slimming was seen as bad.

How they achieved this

- From 1933, many women were forced to leave their jobs as doctors, lawyers and teachers. Employers were told to favour men.
- To encourage women to have large families, the government offered medals to reward women for the number of children they had. Gold was given for eight children, silver for six and bronze for five.
- They used the power of propaganda to persuade women to follow their ideals, using leaflets, newspapers and films.
- Local wardens would report women who were not following Nazi ideas. This made it difficult for women who dressed fashionably or smoked to do so in public.
- Women's organisations were set up by the Nazis, such as the Nazi Women's League. They used propaganda to encourage women to embrace the Three Ks.

The success of the policies

✔ The birth rate in Germany increased between 1933 and 1939.

✔ In the early 1930s, the number of married women in employment fell.

✔ Around 6 million women joined the Nazi women's organisations, which many found rewarding.

✗ The number of women workers actually increased between 1933 and 1939 because the economy was doing very well and many women did not want to give up their jobs.

✗ Employers hired more women because their wages were lower than men's wages.

✗ Most married Germans still only had an average of two children per family.

Revision task

Write two paragraphs of text to explain:

1. the Nazi view of the role of women in society

2. the methods they used to force women to conform to this.

Source A: A Nazi poster from 1938. The caption reads 'NSDAP [The National Socialist Party] will save the people's community; fellow-countrymen, if you need advice and help, apply to the local branches'

The woman is wearing simple clothing and has her hair tied back. This suggests …

The woman in the image is holding a baby. This suggests that her role was to have a family and look after the children.

Exam practice

1. What can you learn from Source A about the role of women in Nazi Germany?
   (4 marks)

Answers online

Nazi policies towards young people

Revised

What the Nazis wanted

- To control the youth of Germany and make them grow up loyal to the government.
- To train young girls as homemakers and boys as workers or soldiers.

How they achieved this

Schools

- New subjects were introduced such as Race Studies that taught pupils about how superior the German race was and how other races were inferior.
- Only German history was taught in schools. The history was rewritten to support Nazi ideas, depicting the Jews and communists as evil. History textbooks were also rewritten.
- Boys were taught mostly science, military drill and maths in order to prepare them for life in work or the armed forces.

- Girls were taught subjects that would suit their role as homemakers in the future such as needlework and domestic science.

The Hitler Youth

- Girls joined the League of German Maidens and were taught domestic chores such as cleaning, cooking and raising children. They also did physical training to prepare them for motherhood.
- Boys, on the other hand, could join the Hitler Youth. Activities included camping, war games, rifle training and cross country marching. This was all useful preparation for the armed forces.

Revision task

Create a memory map to show how women and young people were affected by the policies of the Nazi Party. Try to use pictures or diagrams to show your thinking and include benefits and drawbacks for the different people.

The success of the policies

✔ Activities in the Hitler Youth kept lots of young people happy and physically fit.

✔ Many young people developed good friendships with others in the group.

✗ In spite of the activities, around one in five Germans never joined.

✗ Other groups like the Edelweiss Pirates (see page 121) used to clash with the Hitler Youth and fights were common between them.

✗ Some of those who did join found the focus on military drill and obedience off-putting.

✗ Some parents were worried about family life as young people were made to swear allegiance to Hitler before them!

✗ During the war the Hitler Youth were called upon to undertake mundane tasks such as collecting scrap metal. This only added to its unpopularity for some young people.

How the war affected policies towards women and young people

Revised

Women

Attitudes towards women were confusing during the Second World War. The Nazis still believed that only unmarried working-class women should be employed, yet the realities of war meant they needed women to work in factories. The focus of the DFW/NSF (the National Socialist Women's Organisation) changed from 'women as mothers' to 'women as important members in the war effort'. This included organising women's work in munitions factories, instructing women in feeding families on rations and assisting in the evacuation of children.

Young people

All members of society were expected to help in the war effort and this included young people. Many boys and girls worked on farms and helped in other areas of the war effort, including evacuation, fire-fighting and looking after young children. Older members of the Hitler Youth received military training and some boys as young as thirteen were used as soldiers by the end of the war. Those who did not join the Hitler Youth were increasingly seen as acting against the state and were treated very harshly. This included those groups who actively opposed the Nazis, such as the Edelweiss Pirates.

13.2 Economic changes

Nazi economic policies aimed to reduce unemployment within Germany and build up industry so that Germany could become self-sufficient. The Nazis wanted to be in the position where they did not have to rely on other countries to import raw materials and other goods. They were particularly focused on building up the arms industry so that they could be ready for war. The way the Nazis controlled the workforce helped to fulfil these policies. However, the policies did not succeed in making Germany self-sufficient.

> **Key content**
> - Policies for reducing unemployment
> - The effect of Nazi economic policies
> - The effect of war on economic policies

Policies for reducing unemployment

Revised

Hjalmar Schacht's 'New Plan' (1933–37) and Hermann Göring's 'Four-Year Plan' (1936–39) reduced unemployment by:

- starting a huge building programme to create new motorways (autobahns), hospitals and houses
- re-arming Germany, creating millions of jobs in ammunition factories
- increasing the armed forces to 1,400,000
- forcing all young men between the ages of 18 and 25 to work
- removing women and Jews from the employment register to make the figures look better.

The effect of Nazi economic policies

Revised

Workers

1. As there were no trade unions, all workers joined the Nazi-created German Labour Front (DAF). This group was supposed to negotiate rights for workers …	But →	… the Labour Front often supported employers who wanted lower wages and increased working hours.
2. The DAF set up the 'Strength through Joy' programme that organised holidays and other leisure activities for workers and families. The Nazis believed that happy workers would work harder for them …	But →	… in reality not many holidays were organised and usually the rewards consisted of cheap cinema and theatre tickets.
3. The 'Beauty of Labour' scheme was set up to improve working conditions. It did negotiate some improvements such as better lunches and toilet facilities …	But →	… many workers did not like the scheme as these improvements were expected to be made by them in their spare time!

Farmers

Farmers had supported the Nazis enthusiastically. They benefited from the regime as Hitler guaranteed high food prices and offered them security if they fell behind on their rent …	But →	… work schemes encouraged many people to head for the towns to seek better wages and so farmers found it increasingly hard to find workers in the countryside.

The effect of war on economic policies

Revised

Rationing was introduced as soon as war broke out, although shortages did not really affect people for the first two years of war. From 1942 onwards Germany put more and more resources into its unsuccessful war against the USSR. It restricted shops from opening and directed factories to make things needed for the war effort rather than things for civilians. By the end of the war there were extreme shortages of food for most people.

A black market existed outside of the rationing system and was exploited by some Germans.

Heavy bombing of German cities resulted in huge casualties. Many homes were destroyed, which meant German citizens needed re-housing. There was looting and crime increased in some areas as citizens tried to survive the food shortages and Allied bombings.

13.3 The Nazi views on minorities

Hitler wrote and spoke about his views of different races and nationalities from the early 1920s. Once in power, he was able to act on his beliefs by passing numerous laws that affected millions of people in Germany and her conquered countries.

The Nazis acted in a brutal way towards certain minority groups. Laws and violence were used to control these *Untermenschen*. As the Second World War progressed, the Nazis turned to more deadly methods of dealing with these unwanted peoples – death camps.

> **Key term**
>
> *Untermenschen* – means sub humans. This is what the Nazis called other races including Jews and Eastern Europeans.

Key content

- What the Nazis believed about race
- How the Nazis viewed minority groups
- Nazi treatment of Jews between 1933 and 1945
- The Final Solution

What the Nazis believed about race

Revised ☐

The Nazis believed that the German people were the master race (**Aryan**), and that Aryans were superior to all others races. Hitler believed that he could make this master race by carefully breeding those people who had the features of an Aryan, including blonde hair and blue eyes. Germans who fitted this description were encouraged to marry and have children.

> **Key term**
>
> **Aryan** – the Aryan people were a race of people thought to originate from Scandinavia and had features that included blonde hair and blue eyes. They were also tall and athletic in build.

How the Nazis viewed minority groups

Revised ☐

The Nazis wanted to remove all those who were a drain on German society or who did not contribute or conform to their ideal. Some of these groups included the following.

- **People with a disability:** The Nazis believed that having a disability was a disease that could be passed on from generation to generation. At first they sterilised people with a disability and mentally ill people. Then, during the war, they began to secretly murder them in specialised hospitals.
- **Gypsies:** They were viewed by the Nazis as a problem because they were not Aryan, moved around too often and did not hold down a steady job. Many Gypsies were sent to concentration camps.
- **Black people:** They were dealt with in a similar way to Jews. Marriages between Germans and black people were made illegal. Furthermore, children already born from a mixed race couple were sterilised.

Nazi treatment of Jews between 1933 and 1945

Revised

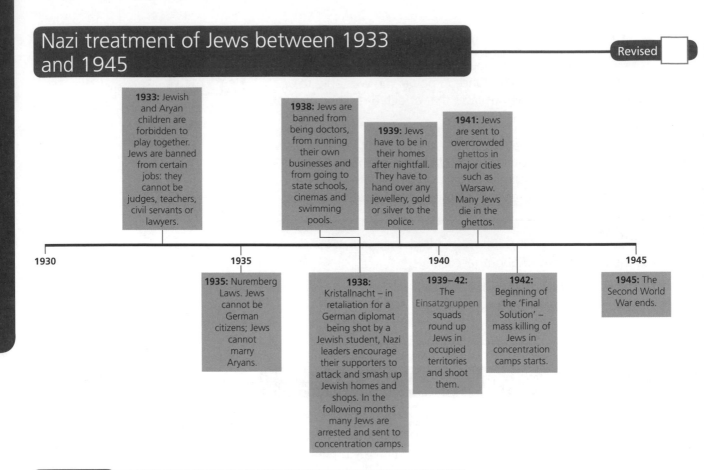

1933: Jewish and Aryan children are forbidden to play together. Jews are banned from certain jobs: they cannot be judges, teachers, civil servants or lawyers.

1938: Jews are banned from being doctors, from running their own businesses and from going to state schools, cinemas and swimming pools.

1939: Jews have to be in their homes after nightfall. They have to hand over any jewellery, gold or silver to the police.

1941: Jews are sent to overcrowded ghettos in major cities such as Warsaw. Many Jews die in the ghettos.

1930　　　　　　1935　　　　　　1940　　　　　　1945

1935: Nuremberg Laws. Jews cannot be German citizens; Jews cannot marry Aryans.

1938: Kristallnacht – in retaliation for a German diplomat being shot by a Jewish student, Nazi leaders encourage their supporters to attack and smash up Jewish homes and shops. In the following months many Jews are arrested and sent to concentration camps.

1939–42: The Einsatzgruppen squads round up Jews in occupied territories and shoot them.

1942: Beginning of the 'Final Solution' – mass killing of Jews in concentration camps starts.

1945: The Second World War ends.

Key terms

Einsatzgruppen – special SS units that followed behind the regular German army into countries like Poland and the Ukraine. They rounded up Jews in towns, made them dig trenches and then shot them so they fell in.

Ghettos – walled off sections in cities in Poland, Czechoslovakia and Lithuania in which Jews were contained. These ghettos were overcrowded with cramped conditions and there was little food or basic services. Hundreds of Jews died each day in these places.

The Final Solution

Revised

What was it? As more countries came under German occupation during the Second World War, the Nazis realised their methods of solving the 'Jewish Problem' (killing Jews) with the Einsatzgruppen and the use of ghettos was inefficient. In 1942, at the Wannsee Conference, top Nazi leaders decided that they needed a way to kill people in large numbers. They decided to build special camps to do this. This would be the Final Solution to the Jewish problem.

Where? The Nazis built camps in Germany and other occupied countries. Treblinka and Auschwitz were two of the most well-known death camps.

How did they do it? When the Nazis took over a country, they drew up a list of Jews and then arrested and transported them to the camps. On arrival, Nazi doctors decided who was fit enough to work and who was to go straight to the gas chambers. Up to 2000 people at once could be killed in a gas chamber.

What was the outcome? At the end of the Second World War, the Nazis had murdered around 6 million Jews and other minorities and around 4 million Russian prisoners.

Revision task

Using the timeline and the information above, draw a graph to sum up how the Nazi treatment of the Jews changed from 1933 to 1945. Add notes to your graph to help you remember the important events.

Exam practice

1. Describe the importance of Kristallnacht (Night of the Broken Glass), November 1938. **(9 marks)**

Answers online